For Those in Peril

A Call for the Church to Speak Truth to the State

CHARLIE RODRIGUEZ
with Paula Rodriguez

For Those in Peril
A Call for the Church to Speak Truth to the State

CHARLIE RODRIGUEZ
with Paula Rodriguez

FOR THOSE IN PERIL: A Call for the Church to Speak Truth to the State. Copyright 2021 by Charlie Rodriguez. All rights reserved.
Printed in the United States of America. No part of this book may be used or reproduced in any manner whatsoever without written permission except in the case of brief quotations embodied in critical articles or reviews.
For information, contact Tanglewood Group at:
https://www.tanglewoodpublishing.org/contact.html

FIRST EDITION

ISBN 978-1-7345087-6-5

CONTENTS

Historical Introduction..................5
Eternal Father, Strong to Save 7
Introduction........................9
1. Stolen.........................13
2. A Charge Against the Church..........17
3. A Charge To the Church.............21
4. How Did This Happen?..............27
5. But What About Prayer?.............31
6. Living on the "Dark Side"............35
7. The Spirituality of the Church.........39
8. Traditionalism...................45
9. The Critical Necessity of Common Grace...49
10. Pharisees Then and Now............57
11. Christians and Politics.............61
12. Silence and Lukewarmness..........65
13. Accurately Handle the Word of Truth....73
14. Never Take a Back Seat............77
15. Critical Theory..................89
16. Seek Mature Christian Wisdom......105
17. The Moral Obligation to Resist Unlawful Government.......113
18. "When the Dogma Lives Loudly" by Archbishop Emeritus
    of Philadelphia Charles J. Chaput.....117
Conclusion.......................121
Appendix........................123
   Letter to a Mega-Church Pastor, Charlie Rodriguez..........124
   10 Reasons Why the Church Should Not Abandon Politics,
    Jerry Newcombe..............127
   The Prayer of a Weary Black Woman – Vistas in Woke Theology,
    Billy Otten.................132
   Preface to *Common Grace*.............137
   Common Grace, Louis Berkhof..........138
Bibliography......................168

HISTORICAL INTRODUCTION

Rear Admiral William D. Rodriguez

It is an honor for me to write this short introduction to Reverend Charlie Rodriguez' book with regard to his use of the USS CONSTITUTION pictured on the cover. The USS CONSTITUTION—"Old Ironsides"—has become a symbol of our Navy's strength and courage. Her proud and lasting history is well published and well known, especially to those of us who served in our Navy. For over 223 years, she has served our Navy and our country well, and today, her mission is to promote understanding of the Navy's role in war and peace through active participation in public events and education through outreach programs, public access, and historic demonstration. The USS CONSTITUTION continued throughout her gallant service to our nation protecting the interests and the ethos of our country.

During her time at sea, in numerous battles and other engagements, the USS CONSTITUTION became the beacon of not only strength and courage, but of faith and hope during the days when our country was growing and taking its place in the world. She and her Sailors were strong and fearless, and with their faith in God and what our country stood for, she and her crew persevered. Because of her construction of hard New England Oak, her nickname was aptly coined during one of the great battles during the War of 1812 when the USS CONSTITUTION captured the British ship HMS GUERRIERE. A sailor on the HMS GUERRIERE saw 18-pound British cannonballs bouncing right off the hull of the USS CONSTITUTION and exclaimed, "Huzza, her sides are made of iron!"

Reverend Charlie Rodriguez appropriately states, "In matters of morality, the Christian Church should navigate THE SHIP OF THE STATE." Sailors at sea have always been God-fearing with a special bond to each other, the sea and their country. Throughout the history of the USS CONSTITUTION, her crew, through their faith in God and the mighty ship in which they commanded were akin to the Christian Church that navigated the "Ship of the State". In the days when trade and commerce, as well as national pride, was executed at sea, the USS CONSTITUTION projected the very being of our new country. The crew and their ship fought off those very foes of our new nation who were determined to undermine our morals and our very foundation on which our country was built upon. With resounding success, the USS CONSTITUTION became that beacon that represented everything that was good, moral and Godly about the United States of America.

Rear Admiral William D. Rodriguez,
United States Navy, Retired

ETERNAL FATHER, STRONG TO SAVE

Eternal Father, strong to save,
Whose arm hath bound the restless wave,
Who bid'st the mighty ocean deep
Its own appointed limits keep;
O hear us when we cry to thee,
For those in peril on the sea.

O Christ, Whose voice the waters heard
And hushed their raging at Thy word,
Who walked'st on the foaming deep,
And calm amidst its rage dids't sleep;
Oh hear us when we cry to Thee
For those in peril on the sea!

Most Holy Spirit! Who didst brood
Upon the chaos dark and rude,
And bid its angry tumult cease,
And give, for wild confusion, peace;
Oh hear us when we cry to Thee
For those in peril on the sea!

O Trinity of love and power!
Our brethren shield in danger's hour;
From rock and tempest, fire and foe,
Protect them wheresoe'er they go;
Thus evermore shall rise to Thee,
Glad hymns of praise from land and sea.

Ⓢ This work is in the public domain in its country of origin and other countries and areas where the copyright term is the author's life plus 100 years or fewer.

The hymn "Eternal Father, Strong to Save" was originally written by a clergyman of the Church of England, the Reverend William Whiting. Reverend Whiting (1825–1878) had survived a terrible storm in the Mediterranean Sea, and this experience led him to write the hymn. The words were set to music by the Reverend John B. Dykes. In later years, the hymn came to have special meaning to men and women serving in the navies of many countries, and it has come to be known as the "Navy Hymn." As more branches of service developed, alternate verses were written to encompass all spheres of military life.[1]

---

[1] "Navy Music." n.p.

INTRODUCTION

The citizens of the United States are in peril. The rights that we have taken for granted for over two hundred years are being threatened. Our nation's founding on a proper understanding of God's Moral Law is being eroded. Our country's foundation on the rock has been downgraded to sand. But rather than wring our hands as though there is no hope, we must ask what we can do, especially those of us who follow Christ. Can the Church correct the course of the State? It is our belief that it can.

We must begin with the fundamental question: Who defines morality: God or the State? If it is the State (one, or more than one, branch of government), then morality is subjectively determined and can be whatever the State wants it to be. If it is God, who has given us His holy, inerrant, and infallible Word, then the definition of morality is objective and independent of human understanding.

The State may reject the objective and independent evidence of God's Moral Law, but it can never say that it doesn't exist;

just as we cannot say, because we despise its philosophy, that *The Communist Manifesto* doesn't exist. It does exist. In fact, we own a copy. Likewise, as William Wilberforce said, "You may choose to look the other way, but you can never say again that you didn't know." [2]

Our argument for the Church speaking openly about the State's violation of the Moral Law is not just an academic exercise. For if in truth we believe that God alone defines morality and that we are commanded to teach <u>all</u> His truth (unlike Tomas Jefferson did in his edited Bible), then we must "Do our best to present ourselves to God as one approved, a worker who has no need to be ashamed, rightly handling the word of truth" (2 Tim. 2:15, ESV). In other words, we have an obligation to interpret God's Word correctly, especially during times when it is misinterpreted corporately by the State.

Some in the Church may want to continue "quarreling about words" (2 Tim. 2:14a), in other words, arguing about petty matters; but this causes the weightier matters (e.g., usurpation of the Moral Law by the State) to go unattended, thus obscuring the identity of a more deadly enemy: an autonomous, arrogant, spiritually blind, and dangerous State, who declares it is her right, and not God's, to define morality. Pastor Ray Stedman illustrated it this way:

"As the Battle of Trafalgar was about to begin, Admiral Nelson came across two officers of his own flagship who were arguing hotly and about to take sword to each other. Nelson

---

[2] Strom, p. 225.

stepped between them and said, 'Stop.' Then, pointing to the French fleet, he said, 'There is the enemy.'" [3]

For whatever reason, if the Church refuses to speak about the State's usurpation of God's Moral Law and chooses to "dispute about words" instead, then by default it grants permission to the State to define morality for everyone. But even in the Church's sinful silence, the Holy Spirit is relentless to communicate His truth to us by way of example and illustration, and to spare us all the consequences of corporate sin (i.e., when the State legislates immorality).

From a human perspective, it is predictable, though not biblical, that the Church would resist speaking to the State about its blatant contempt of God's Moral Law. However, that fact does not make the consequences of silence any less serious--to the Church or to the general public. In the following chapters, we will analyze why the Church refuses to act and why that refusal is so detrimental to Christian society and to society at large.

We will discuss reasons why the Church has failed to speak out. We will examine the doctrine of Common Grace, an extremely important Christian doctrine which should be part of Church instruction at all age levels. However, most churches are only vaguely familiar with what the Bible teaches about how an orderly life is made possible, how the destructive power of sin is restrained, and many other blessings given by God which benefit everyone.

---
3 Stedman, n.p.

It is also important to understand how differing views of **Kingdom Theology** confuse the biblical view of church and state. For instance, if your pastor studied at Reformed Theological Seminary rather than Westminster Seminary California, there would definitely be a difference in the way this doctrine is taught, and how that affects the understanding of church/state relations. Gets confusing, doesn't it? Actually, the difference hits at the heart of the issue I am addressing-- whether or not the Church should speak to the State about its violations of the Moral Law.

Also, whether we realize it or not, most Christians are affected by both **Traditionalism** and **Tradition**. Traditionalism, as described by Charles Swindoll is "an attitude that resists change, adaptation, or alteration." [4] Tradition, although sharing an appreciation of the past, does not share that "resistance to change, adaptation, or alteration." Put another way by historian Jaroslav Pelikan: Tradition is the living faith of the dead; traditionalism is the dead faith of the living. And, I suppose I should add, it is traditionalism that gives tradition such a bad name." [5]

The question of who defines morality, God or State, should not be complicated, especially for the Church; but for various reasons, many in the Church today are part of the problem rather than the solution. The Church has become comfortable, and that's exactly where the Devil wants us to be.

---

4   Swindoll, n.p.
5   Pelikan, p. 65.

CHAPTER 1

STOLEN

In 1941, a portrait of Adele Bloch-Bauer was stolen by the Nazis from Austrian banker Ferdinand Bloch-Bauer and displayed at the Österreichische Galerie Belvedere in Vienna. After a long international court battle, the painting was finally returned to Maria Altmann, Bloch-Bauer's niece, in 2006.

In 2016, Smithsonian Magazine featured an article about the oldest-known carving of the moral code, or Ten Commandments, shared by Judaism, Christianity, and Islam alike. Although this archaeological treasure has not yet been stolen, its contents, God's Moral Law, have been.

Governments and lawmakers regularly steal from God His Moral Law in order to redefine it their own selfish purposes.

Nevertheless, the Moral Law "forever binds all people to obedience and respect of God who gave it" (Westminster Confession of Faith 19:5). [6]

Also stolen is the conscience of man through subterfuge by elitists and progressives in government, media, tech industries, academia, and religious organizations. These entities have taken what is holy and made it profane. They have tricked men and women into believing lies, rather than the truth. They have done this even within the context of the church.

Consider the burgeoning popularity of "Progressive Christianity." According to Michael Kruger, Ph.D., "Progressives have a low view of Christ; are focused on moralism, not salvation; downplay fallenness and are intolerant of historic Christianity." [7] Their goal is to be the conscience of man, rather than our own God-given knowledge of the law, written on our hearts, which should lead us to repentance and faith in Christ.

God's Moral Law is best summarized in the Ten Commandments and fulfilled by loving your neighbor as yourself (Rom. 13:9), and governments can and should use these laws in governing, but their origin is with a Holy God who alone defines them. Redefining God's Moral Law (e.g., when governments say abortion is not murder, that there are more than two genders, that you may change your gender, that marriage can be anything you want it to

---

6   *Confessions of Our Faith*, p. 32.
7   Kruger, n.p.

be, etc.) is, in essence, stealing from God. In a court of law, it would be deemed plagiarism, and restitution would be in order.

Restitution is defined by *American Jurisprudence* as the "return or restoration of a specific thing or condition." [8] If the Church and Government began to think in legal terms-- such as restoring God's Moral Law to its original meaning-- perhaps the conscience of both will be pricked. It is a method that Nathan used with David ("You are the man!") and one approved by God.

Remember the movie "Walk the Line" about Johnny Cash, and the scene with producer Sam Phillips?

> **Sam Phillips:** We've already heard that song a hundred times. Just like that. Just... like... how... you... sing it.
> **Johnny Cash:** Well you didn't let us bring it home.
> **Sam Phillips:** Bring... bring it home? All right, let's bring it home. If you was hit by a truck and you was lying out there in that gutter dying, and you had time to sing *one* song. Huh? One song that people would remember before you're dirt. One song that would let God know how you felt about your time here on Earth. One song that would sum you up. You tellin' me that's the song you'd sing? That same Jimmy Davis tune we hear on the radio all day . . .or would you sing somethin' different. Somethin' real.

---
[8]   Bordeau, n.p.

Somethin' you felt. Cause I'm telling you right now, that's the kind of song people want to hear. [9]

There are three important points in this scene. First, Sam's honesty. Second, Johnny's willingness to listen and follow Sam's advice. Third, the expression on Sam's face when he hears Johnny sing it differently and not just the way "it's supposed to be sung."

What about sermons regarding **State violations**, in contrast to **Individual violations**, of God's Moral Law? Are you hearing these messages in Church, and are they "somethin' different"? They need to be, especially for the sake of the children. Because unless children have biblically wise and available parents, the only other place for this information is the Church.

I have examined hundreds of beautiful church websites and their wonderful programs (Sunday school, discipleship, weekly Bible studies for all ages, choir, world and local missions, prayer groups, counseling). Unfortunately, I was not able to find even one with an emphasis on such a serious Church matter as: VIOLATIONS OF GOD'S MORAL LAW BY THE STATE. The Moral Law must never be understood and defined by politicians. That is the role of the Church; and until the Church accepts responsibility to publicly defend and define the Moral Law, nothing will change.

---

9   Dennis, n.p.

CHAPTER 2

A CHARGE AGAINST THE CHURCH

Whenever the subject of Church and State is mentioned, a certain bias appears, almost out of nowhere, favoring "separation." Although it seems to be a natural reaction, it is neither Biblical nor Constitutional. "Separation of church and state" is an enabler of the sinfulness of seeking independence from God and of redefining the Moral Law. Without thinking of the implications of their actions, many church, academic, and political leaders guide the public away from God when they espouse the oft-repeated phrase "separation of church and state."

The biblical antidote to the State's interpretation and advocacy of its own Moral Law is to stir the conscience of right and wrong behavior (e.g., "Go and sin no more," [John 8:11] and "You are the man!" [II Samuel 12:7]). Though knowledge of right and wrong is part of our spiritual DNA, it must be repeatedly taught because the "law is our schoolmaster to bring us unto Christ" (Gal. 3:24). And because the Christian Church is the repository of God's truth, it is necessary that the Church assume this responsibility of advocacy and interpretation. In the past, these stirrings of the conscience, or Awakenings, had the potential to move whole nations from bad government to good government through an evangelistic appeal to both Law and Grace. Surely, it can happen again in our day.

Along the same lines, if so-called *social issues* are truly biblical/moral issues, then they belong within the *original jurisdiction* of the Church, rather than being assigned to the State, as understood in a Lutheran "two-kingdom" or Presbyterian "spirituality of the church doctrine" jurisdiction. (These doctrines will be discussed later in this work.) Consequently, the Church, by the use of its very powerful gifts of proclamation and interpretation, is foundational for the correct understanding of law and order and good government which should be advanced by good magistrates.

Impossible for the Church to do in our day? No, but it does take faith, hard work, and a willingness to work together. It is also the power of God's Word that is the driving force. Like Jesus, we must choose our words very carefully when speaking to select leaders and groups like the Pharisees and their advocates today, who seek to steal original jurisdiction over the Moral Law away from the Church.

Some will say that some of the words of Christ such as, "Woe to you!" (Matthew 23) are too harsh and should not be used by His followers today. Jesus' words were a powerful and harsh rebuke to those who were attempting to usurp the Moral authority of God. "Woe to you!," if used today to speak to similar leaders, is imitating Christ—in style and in substance. Furthermore, Jesus never taught "separation of church and state," if that is the only argument used not to speak.

A critical question for the Church, in any age, is precisely this: If grievous violations of God's Moral Law are voted into law, do Church leaders really understand the magnitude of that evil? C.S. Lewis reminds us that it is much more sinister than we think:

> The greatest evil is not now done in those sordid "dens of crime" that Dickens loved to paint. It is not done even in concentration camps and labor camps. In those we see its final result. But it is conceived and ordered (moved, seconded, carried, and recorded) in clean, carpeted, warmed and well-lighted offices, by quiet men with white collars and cut fingernails and smooth-shaven cheeks who do not need to raise their voices.[10]

What about today? Who are these "quiet men" (and women) whose evil is conceived and ordered in clean and well-lighted offices?" If we are honest and alert, we know the answer

---
[10]   Lewis, p. xxxvii

because we know how liberal legislators vote, and we know Party platforms. It is to Congress, one of the most powerful (but no longer august) legislative bodies in world history, that the Church, and not just the individual, must appeal. Jesus is not intimidated by secular legislation and neither should the Church be. Jesus would remind us to abide by the law (if it is not immoral), but He would never tell us to be silent when the Moral Law is breached by the State.

The reality is that some Church leaders do not see a clear Biblical path, as Jesus did, warranting them to speak to the State about corporate sin. In light of this, in the next few chapters, I will attempt to shine the light of Scripture and history upon the Church's responsibilities in this area.

Finally, as contrary thoughts appear, suddenly and joltingly, making us uncertain, fearful, impotent, and speechless concerning a State's legislative action against the Moral Law, we must resist "giving the Devil a foothold." On earth we will always be in the middle of spiritual battles. Our duty is to accept that reality and engage the enemy relentlessly in order to "curb the destructive power of sin, maintaining in a measure the moral order of the universe, thus making an orderly life possible." [11]

---

[11] Berkhof, pp. 432-444

CHAPTER 3

A CHARGE TO THE CHURCH

So why does the Church still resist speaking to the State about its corporate violations of God's Moral Law? From my research, I have found ten reasons for Church resistance to speaking out against the State when it overturns the Moral Law through its legislative power:

1. The Church resists because it does not see its duty to speak about State violations of the Moral Law.

2. The Church resists because it is in a state of denial.

3. The Church resists because of a misunderstanding of separation of Church and State.

4. The Church resists because it does not fully understand the doctrine of Common Grace.

5. The Church resists because it lacks understanding of the corporate nature of sin.

6. The Church resists because of confusion over Kingdom Theology.

7. The Church resists because speaking to the State is not a priority.

8. The Church resists because of Traditionalism.

9. The Church resists because its focus has been blurred.

10. The Church resists because the older model it uses does not include a response from the Church when the State overturns the Moral Law.

In matters which may seem difficult, who does the Church follow or imitate? Consider Jesus and Paul, if you will, who harshly criticized the Pharisees and Sadducees (Jewish political and religious leaders) and Judaizers (Jewish Christian leaders) for misrepresenting and distorting the Moral Law. Two thousand years changes nothing. Of course, the dominant focus of moral issues has changed (abortion, marriage, gender dysphoria, etc.); nevertheless, it is still corporate misrepresentation and distortion of the Moral Law, and the Church is morally obliged to respond to it.

Paul said, "Imitate me just as I imitate Christ." The Church should confront those who distort the Moral Law just as Christ did in Matthew 23 ("Woe to you, scribes and Pharisees, hypocrites! For you tithe mint and dill and cumin, and have neglected the weightier matters of the law: justice and mercy and faithfulness") and as Paul did when he spoke boldly to King Agrippa (Acts 26:24-29).

When we do imitate Paul and Christ, this is what should happen, and this is what we should see with our own eyes: church leaders becoming so convicted concerning State misrepresentations and distortions of the Moral Law, that they actually begin to preach and develop educational programs in this area for all age levels. This is especially important for children who are daily confronted with opposing views.

If corporate or national sin is not a part of a church's vocabulary and teaching, it should be. Throughout history there are very good reasons why God chooses to remove His restraining Grace (the work of the Holy Spirit in restraining human sin) from an entire nation. When this happens, that nation is no longer a safe place. Yes, there will always be individual sin that we will have to contend with in this life, but Common Grace benefits everyone—believer and nonbeliever alike—by favoring mankind with kindness and love through law and order, protection, peace, and happiness. As Jesus says in Matthew 5:45, "For he makes his sun rise on the evil and on the good, and sends rain on the just and on the unjust."

But Common Grace comes with a price: Government must never take the place of God, it must never overthrow God's

Moral Law, and it is the duty of the Church to teach the blessings of obedience and the tragedy of disobedience.

What I propose to the Church and para-church organizations regarding the State's corporate sin is: (1) a shift in focus, encompassing a broader view of Scripture ("teaching them to observe all things I have commanded" [Matthew 28:20]); and (2) a new model, radically different from the older church/state model, which never encouraged speaking directly to the State as a corporate body when it overturns the Moral Law.

To put it in context, the meaning of "speaking to the State," in the modern sense, ordinarily means the advocacy of a very general *Christian world and life view*. What is unique in this is how united church and para-church groups are in defending their biblical and Constitutional rights. But this unity does not extend to confronting the misinterpretation of the Moral Law by the state. That, in their minds, would be engaging in the political. What was sidelined in this process, unfortunately, was the moral authority of the Church, because the Church itself did not resist intrusion by the State. Like Luther, who taught a doctrine of two kingdoms, they have encouraged *individuals* to respond to the State, but not the *Church* as a body. Similarly, American Presbyterianism's "spirituality doctrine" has also silenced the Church, while supposedly encouraging the individual to respond on moral issues. Over time, even the individual church member has become silent on the moral issues because the Church has been silent.

Law and order in a civil society depend upon a correct biblical understanding of morality. According to the Bible, this is the way things are supposed to work: The magistrate (national, state, or local leader) exercises judicial authority in God's Kingdom over good and just laws. (Romans 13:1,3: There is no authority except from God, and those that exist have been instituted by God. For rulers are not a terror to good conduct, but to bad.) The Christian Church exercises spiritual authority in the same Kingdom over the definition of morality as given in God's Word. (Matthew 28:20) Same God, same Kingdom, different roles.

Therefore, the Christian Church must be united and resolute in this: The Moral Law of God is not the State's to define. This belongs exclusively to the Christian Church to teach powerfully and winsomely, in and out of church, exactly what the Bible teaches so that hearers will learn to fear God more than man.

So, one of the first steps the Church should take is to reject adherence to traditional views which are not clearly biblical views (traditionalism) and routinely evaluate issues which need to be addressed. I argue that if we do just one thing right regarding Church and State, it should be to speak forcefully with unity when the State violates God's Moral Law. Churches should regularly teach The Moral Law, explain how it is plagiarized by lawmakers and taught to the masses, and argue for "restitution" to its original intent. As Christian Americans, we must be originalists with the Bible as well as the Constitution.

My recommendation is to start with regular Church discussions in this area, tailored to each age group. At the same time, these discussions must be advertised on the Church's website as to time, place, and subject. Violations of the Moral Law are voted into Secular Law every day, so it is never difficult to find a subject. I can assure you, young people have already formed opinions in these areas (some good, some bad). Teaching God's standards should be an ongoing ministry of the Church. It cannot be accomplished in just one sermon a week, but that is a place to start. And if we do this, we will see "justice roll down like waters, and righteousness like an ever-flowing stream" (Amos 5:24).

CHAPTER 4

HOW DID THIS HAPPEN?

In troubling times, we often ask, "How did this happen?" The Church should ask a similar question: "How did we ever get into to a position of not responding to the very clear violations by the State of God's Moral Law in our day?

In this and following chapters, I will discuss some of the most prominent and disturbing reasons for Church silence—disturbing because morality is defined by God, and it is His Church which is the repository of both Word and meaning. However, this has been compromised by:

1. The notion of "Separation of Church and State"
2. The confusion over Kingdom theology

3. The influence of the "Spirituality of the Church" Concept

4. The clinging to Traditionalism

5. The failure to understand Jesus' example in dealing with the Pharisees

This chapter will consider the concept of "Separation of Church and State." The other concepts will be dealt with in subsequent chapters.

By now, the true meaning of the phrase "Separation of Church and State" should be clearly understood and taught regularly in the Church. However, I do not find this to be the case, and I still hear pastors and church members confused by it.

Article 3 of the Bill of Rights states: "Congress shall make no law respecting an establishment of religion, or prohibiting the free exercise thereof." This article was considered to be necessary and important, as it was the first right given to US citizens. In England and other countries from which the founding fathers had come, state religions were common and persecution for not following the state religion was intense. The earliest Congresses felt that it was imperative to ensure that citizens of the new United States were free to pursue whatever religion they chose, without fear of persecution.

Notice that there is no injunction against any church or individual speaking to the state on matters of morality. The only injunction is against the State's interfering in matters of religion. This article has been misquoted and misused until most citizens probably have no idea about what it really says.

The idea of "separation of church and state" came from a letter written by Thomas Jefferson in response to a letter of concern from the Danbury Baptist Association expressing their fear that religious freedom was a matter of permission from the State, rather than an inalienable right. Jefferson used the phrase "wall of separation of church and state" to ensure the Danbury Baptists that it was the intent of the writers of the Bill of Rights to guarantee every citizen the right to pursue whichever religion he or she desired. It in no way allowed the government to interfere with religion or to prohibit religious expression in the public sphere.[12]

This intent of the writers of the Bill of Rights has become so distorted and misused that most Americans use the term "separation of church and state" to mean precisely the opposite of its intended meaning. Most Americans believe that "separation of church and state" requires that the church have no voice or involvement in affairs of state.

In discussing "separation of church and state," we must also consider the Johnson Amendment, which prohibits all 501(c)(3) non-profit organizations from endorsing or opposing individual political candidates. The Amendment

---
12   Lankford and Moore, n.p.

does not prohibit speaking of party platforms or philosophy. Churches and other such organizations are free to distribute information regarding a party's or individual candidate's position on issues. They are only prohibited from specifically endorsing or opposing specific candidates. [13]

However, "let the buyer beware." Some legislators consider teaching what the Bible says about morality as "hate speech," and they would like to prohibit that too. It is the duty of the Church to speak out on moral issues and to continue teaching everything Jesus commanded (Mt. 28:20; Acts 4:20) knowing that "the gates of Hell will not prevail against it." (Mt. 16:19).

Whatever the rationale today—as an individual or a church body—if we still cling to a "Separation of Church and State" concept, we need to remember its unlawful use in the past and how it may still be used today, in some quarters, to foster Church and individual silence when God's Moral Law is being redefined and overturned by the State. Today, the "Separation of Church and State" concept is, by a strange twist of fate, the doctrine of liberals, of the establishment, of statists, of socialists, of terrorist groups, and of all who use it to lend credibility to their cause because they want to play God rather than live by His standards.

---

[13]   Gjelten, n.p.

CHAPTER 5

WHAT ABOUT PRAYER?

There are probably many in the Church who are concerned about things that are happening in our country, and they are probably praying about these things. Prayer is the most powerful weapon a Christian has at his/her disposal. We should always be in prayer. But often, action is also needed. There are many things that we pray about that are truly beyond our control: the illness of a loved one, the need for a job, financial distress. But even in those things, we take action. We take the loved on to a doctor, we apply for jobs, we seek financial counseling. Too often, the phrase, "I'll pray about it" is merely an excuse to do nothing.

Of course, God may be calling an individual to pray earnestly over a given situation. If that is the case, that person will devote much of his or her time to praying about what God has laid on his/her heart. Simply reciting a list of prayer requests is not praying earnestly, and if that is our calling from God, that is not what we will do.

Consider these Scriptures about the need to take action as well as to pray.

> **James 2:14-17:** What good is it, my brothers, if someone says he has faith but does not have works? Can that faith save him? If a brother or sister is poorly clothed and lacking in daily food, and one of you says to them, "Go in peace, be warmed and filled," without giving them the things needed for the body, what good is that? So also faith by itself, if it does not have works, is dead.
>
> **James 1:23-25:** For if anyone is a hearer of the word and not a doer, he is like a man who looks intently at his natural face in a mirror. For he looks at himself and goes away and at once forgets what he was like. But the one who looks into the perfect law, the law of liberty, and perseveres, being no hearer who forgets but a doer who acts, he will be blessed in his doing.
>
> **James 2:18:** But someone will say, "You have faith and I have works." Show me your faith apart from your works, and I will show you my faith by my works.
>
> **I John 3:18:** Little children, let us not love in word or talk but in deed and in truth.

James 4:17: So whoever knows the right thing to do and fails to do it, for him it is sin.

I Peter 1:13: Therefore, preparing your minds for action, and being sober-minded, set your hope fully on the grace that will be brought to you at the revelation of Jesus Christ.

James I:22: But be doers of the word, and not hearers only, deceiving yourselves.

James 2:26: For as the body apart from the spirit is dead, so also faith apart from works is dead.

There are also many examples in the Bible of godly men and women who spoke to the rulers of their day, even at their own risk.

1. Moses did not merely pray that God would deliver the Hebrew people from slavery, he confronted Pharoah. (Exodus 5:1-3)

2. Esther prayed about the safety of her people, but she also spoke to the king, even at the risk of death. (Esther 5:1-8)

3. Daniel, when asked to interpret the handwriting on the wall, did not only pray that King Belshazzar would understand the message, he boldly confronted the king with his sinfulness. (Daniel 5:17-28)

4. Elijah confronted Ahab and predicted a drought because of his sins. (I Kings 17:1)

5. John the Baptist rebuked Herod for his sin of his marriage to Herodias. (Luke 3:19)

6. Peter and John spoke to the rulers, elders, and scribes of Israel refusing to stop preaching the Gospel of Jesus. (Acts 5:1-20)

These are just a few examples, but they point out the need for godly men and women to speak out to their leaders when the need arises.

Yes, prayer is important. It is essential. We should never undertake anything without first bringing our concerns to God. But in addition to prayer, God often calls us to act, to speak out, to prove our faith by our deeds. We believe that this is such a time.

CHAPTER 6

LIVING ON THE "DARK SIDE"

The recent *Star Wars* series of movies has popularized the concept of two competing powers: the "Dark Side" and the "Force." Those who love good and choose to fight against the "Dark Side" are called the "Resistance," and they are aided by "the Force," an unseen power for good. In Star Wars "theology," the two powers are equal. It is possible for either side to win the war. In the movies, the Force has not yet won the war, but it has won many battles. Everyone in the universe is still living under the control of the Dark Side.

Is this the position of the Church? In the view of some, Satan, as prince of the power of the air, has control of the earth and all that is in it. His opposite, the Lord God, has control of the Kingdom of Heaven and of all that is right and good. This view of God and Satan portrays them as equals, fighting over the same individuals. It is "Star Wars theology," with the possibility that either side can win.

But this is not the picture given in Scripture. Satan is not equal with God. He is a being created by God who once enjoyed God's favor. He is pictured as being cast out of Heaven (Luke 10:18), having to ask permission to do harm to Job (Job 2:1-6), and being destined for eternal punishment (Matthew 25:41). The battle between good and evil is ongoing, even though it has already been won.

According to John Frame, "two-kingdom theology teaches that God has divided his Kingdom into two spheres--- one which is spiritual and the other secular. In this view, God taught the spiritual kingdom to live by his written word, the Bible, but to [disregard] what he has revealed in the natural world. But he taught the secular kingdom to arrange its affairs according to his revelation in the natural world, and not to be ruled by the Bible. This view is not taught in the Bible; furthermore it might lead to the secular sphere separating itself from God and forming a separate kingdom.

"There are others, with whom I agree, who believe that Scripture teaches that God has different purposes for the spiritual and secular parts, but that He rules both parts. In both parts, God expects his creatures to live according to his written word, applying its principles to the natural world, in which he also reveals himself."[14]

---

14 Frame, email, Apr 22

I agree with Dr. John Frame in his analysis of a two-kingdom theology when he writes:

"In my view, this division between two spheres is not biblical. Scripture does not limit the church's authority to a sacred sphere, or the state's authority to the secular. Rather, the limits on church authority, and the limits on state authority, are simply the limits on these institutions indicated in Scripture." [15]

Although Dr. Frame has written much on this subject, when he states that the limits on church and state are set by Scripture, I am convinced that is the most important thing we need to know on this subject. Many want to reach outside of the bounds of Scripture to validate their understanding, but that is the cause of so much unnecessary "quarreling over words" 2 Tim. 2:14) as Paul writes to Timothy.

Just think for a moment how many problems are associated with a 2-kingdom or sphere view:

1. According to a two-kingdom view, the state may, without question from the Church, redefine the Moral Law. Advocates of this view seem to think that they may remain silent when God's Moral Law is being trampled upon. Where does their understanding come from? Certainly not from Scripture, which they profess to believe.

---
15   Frame, email, Mar 18

2. According to a two-kingdom view, the state may defund the police thereby ushering in lawlessness, and the Church must remain silent. Our Lord is, and always has been, the architect of law and order and proclaiming "peace among people of good will" (Luke 2:14). It is only sinful men and women who pervert His justice and good will and usher in His wrath, especially where there is corporate sin (especially among lawmakers) which encourage all to disobey when by a vote they proclaim "evil good, and good evil" (Is. 5:20)

3. According to a two-kingdom view, the state may perjure itself, but the Church must remain silent. No leader of the people is justified in daily violating the 9th Commandment. Do these leaders have no shame before God. Do they not understand that even little children have a sacred conscience which must be protected and nourished? Do they not understand that there are biblical prohibitions against leading little children astray? If they do not, then it must be the mission of the Church to warn them as Christ taught His disciples: "It would be better for him if a millstone were hung around his neck and he were cast into the sea than that he should cause one of these little ones to sin." (Luke 17:2)

CHAPTER 7

THE SPIRITUALITY OF THE CHURCH

Growing out of the two-kingdom doctrine, the concept of the Spirituality of the Church was developed in large part to provide pastors with a legitimate excuse to avoid speaking on certain moral issues, particularly the issue of slavery. Basically, it states that the Church should speak only about spiritual issues and should leave "secular" issues to the government.

This concept became very popular before and during the Civil War due to the reluctance of Southern pastors to deal with the issue of slavery. Most Southern churches were financially at the mercy of rich landowners, whose livelihood depended on the labor of slaves. Plantation owners could not afford to pay their laborers and still live in the lifestyle to which they had become accustomed, hence, the slave trade flourished.

While many Southern pastors probably saw the evils of slavery and would have liked to speak out, their own livelihoods depended on the very landowners against whom they wanted to speak. So, the Spirituality of the Church provided them a way of escape, although not a biblical way. By contending that as pastors, they should limit themselves to spiritual issues, they could avoid speaking about the social evils of the day and still maintain a relatively clear conscience.

Unfortunately, this concept has continued on into the present day. If the church is to concern itself with spiritual matters only, pastors do not need to take possibly unpopular stances against racial prejudice and discrimination and other such divisive issues. This position has allowed racial discrimination to flourish long past its "prime," that is, long after we all knew better.

Reformed Church Historian Sean Michael Lucas makes some very important points regarding the proponents of the "Spirituality of the Church" concept. Lucas's words are in italics:[16]

- *The root of the spirituality of the church doctrine was the separation of church and state* [or two-kingdom approach]. I find it amazing that a prominent Reformed theologian would write so clearly on this; however, this only opens the way for further discussion and questions—

---

16   Lucas, n.p.

in seminaries, in church, in bible studies, and at home. For instance,

1. Was this doctrine at all "spiritual"?
2. Wasn't the original intent of this doctrine to protect powerful church members?
3. Why did it take so long (over 100 years) to cease the teaching of this doctrine?
4. Is there a subtle teaching of it today?
5. Are politicians today being helped by this doctrine?
6. If violations of moral issues are paramount, didn't some liberal churches initially honor God?

- *Such a position demanded silence on matters political and social.* It certainly was understood, even if those words were never uttered. That is why I think children who grow up as children of pastors or elders will fall into one of two camps: Either they more quickly understand this concept than those who did not grow up in the church and are able to come to grips with it and to work to change it, or they have accepted it for years and see no reason to change.

Pastors and church leaders who did not grow up in the church, or who were not aware of underlying church issues, can be surprised and saddened by this concept and may want to make immediate changes. They may not be willing to allow things to change slowly over time.

- *Historically, the "spirituality of the church" concept was invoked to prevent conversations on race while it was involved with education, temperance, or sexual morality.* Most of us have read about Prohibition, and how many people love to say, "you can't legislate morality." But in fact, the State legislates morality all the time. They do it when they pass laws against murder, against theft, against child abuse, etc. They do it when they redefine God's Moral Law. The only difference is that they want Bible-believing Christians to obey them rather than for them to obey God.

- Rather than hiding behind the "spirituality of the church," I feel it is more biblical to say, "Defining the Moral Law is not the job of the State. It belongs exclusively to the Christian church whose solemn duty is to teach what God has given in His Word. It is then the job of the State to enforce those laws which support the Moral Law of God."

- *Peter Slade observed that "the spirituality of the church is in fact the time-tested political strategy of powerful men to perpetuate an unjust status quo free from moral censure...[It] is a sophisticated theological resistance to systemic change: it is not an innocent doctrine misused."* I would agree with Dr. Slade that for some, indeed "it is a sophisticated theological resistance" as I happen to know the powerful man he interviewed when he was writing his dissertation.

- *All of this suggests that southern Presbyterians—the forefathers of the PCA—misunderstood and misapplied what was taught by the Westminster Confession of Faith.* I grew up in the South, and as I grew older, I came to a better understanding of the Bible and of our Confessions. Although many Southern pastors want to honor and revere the church leaders who came before them, we must also be willing to acknowledge their errors and their sins in refusing to stand for God's law and not confronting the issues of their day.

In order to understand how the root of the Spirituality of the Church doctrine provided an excuse and gave the impetus for the disenfranchisement of African-Americans at every level for over a hundred years, read Dr. Lucas' full article, "Owning Our Past," at https://journal.rts.edu/article/owning-our-past-the-spirituality-of-the-church-in-history-failure-and-hope/

CHAPTER 8

TRADITIONALISM

Whether we realize it or not, most Christians are affected by both **Traditionalism** and **Tradition**. Traditionalism, as described by Charles Swindoll is "an attitude that resists change, adaptation, or alteration."[17] Tradition, although sharing an appreciation of the past, does not share that "resistance to change, adaptation, or alteration."

The Christian church has fine traditions, some of which we experience at Christmas and Easter. These traditions, as in my own family, are what have been handed down and some which we have developed on our own.

Most Christian families celebrate Christmas, as do most non-Christian families, and they share certain traditions,

---
17   Swindoll, n.p.

such as the gathering together of family, decorating inside and out, and a festive Christmas meal. Some families have a traditional meal; other like to try new foods and experiences.

When my wife was three years old, her mother was explaining to her that on Christmas, we celebrate Jesus' birthday. Her three-year-old response was, "If it's his birthday, why doesn't he have a birthday cake?" So that year, for the first time, her family celebrated with a birthday cake for Jesus. It was a white cake with white icing, covered with grated coconut, with a single candle in the middle. To this day, over sixty years later, we still make a birthday cake for Jesus, and it still must be a white cake with white icing, covered with grated coconut, with a single candle in the middle. That is the very definition of tradition. In fact, it is probably traditionalism, because according to my wife's family, nothing about that cake is ever allowed to change.

A birthday cake is one thing, but the teaching of the Church is another. Most churches operate out of tradition, and many out of traditionalism—the "we've always done it that way" mentality. Most of us have encountered that type of church. There is no room in those churches for a change in music, for a change in the order of worship, for a change in the serving of communion, or for a change in what is preached. My wife attended a church where she says the only sermon ever preached was about how much God loves us. The words of every sermon were different, but the message was always the same. While we obviously need to know how much God loves us, there is so much more in the Bible that we need to learn.

TRADITIONALISM

Our traditions can be valuable and comforting, and can help to point us to Jesus, but we must be careful to base those traditions on Biblical principles. Otherwise, they can deteriorate into what Jaroslav Pelikan calls "the dead faith of the living." [18]

So how does this relate to the Church speaking to the State about the Moral Law. Simply in this, if we insist on traditionalism, on preaching the same sermons about the same topics week after week, we are not preaching the whole counsel of God. And failure to do that violates the command of God and is therefore sinful.

Pastors must be prepared to speak out against violations of the Moral Law by the State and about political issues of the day, and church congregations must be prepared to hear these things. For a Church Session (or Board, or Diaconate, etc.) to object to such sermons would also be sinful and would amount to leading their flock astray.

Traditions are fine, and can make us feel comfortable and safe, but our goal should not be to feel secure. We can feel secure in God's care for us, but that does not mean that we should be afraid to confront people and issues that have the potential to bring evil down upon us.

There are times to say no, even to tradition. A good example of this is when someone says, in response to speaking to the state about moral issues, that the only responsibility of

---
[18] Pelikan,,

the church is to "win people to Christ, and that will solve all the problems." It may be true that such a philosophy is traditional to many churches, but what is missing is what Christ clearly taught: "If you love me, follow my commandments." (John 14:15).

Jesus did not mean following a set of moral instructions. He meant following all of His commands and teachings. Obviously, we cannot do this perfectly, but as we become more and more like Jesus (which is called Sanctification) we will be able to live lives which are more pleasing to Him. Jesus' greatest commandment is, "Go therefore and make disciples of all nations, baptizing them in the name of the Father and of the Son and of the Holy Spirit, teaching them to observe all that I have commanded you." (Matthew 28:19-20) "All that I have commanded you" surely includes God's Moral Law. If the Church does not teach its members the entirety of the Gospel and the Law, who will?

We must not be afraid to speak out. It is commanded by God, and it is for our own eternal, and perhaps our physical, good. Let us remember the quote from Martin Niemöller: "First they came for the socialists, and I did not speak out—because I was not a socialist. Then they came for the trade unionists, and I did not speak out—because I was not a trade unionist. Then they came for the Jews, and I did not speak out—because I was not a Jew. Then they came for me—and there was no one left to speak for me." [19]

---

[19]   Martin Niemöller, n.p.

CHAPTER 9

THE CRITICAL NECESSITY OF COMMON GRACE

In order to fully appreciate the disastrous consequences of redefining God's Moral Law, we must understand the concept of Common Grace. This chapter will rely heavily on the chapter "Common Grace" from Dr. Louis Berkhof's *Systematic Theology*.

The doctrine of Common Grace as developed by John Calvin describes it as a grace which is given to everyone, which does not pardon or purify us, and does not save anyone. [However] "it restrains the destructive power of sin, maintains in a measure the moral order of the universe, thus making an orderly life possible, distributes in varying degrees gifts and talents among men, promotes the development of science and art, and showers untold blessings upon the children of men."

Most theologians (Calvin, Kuyper, Berkhof, Sproul, Boice, Hodge,) teach God's kindness and loving provision for everyone, or Common Grace, but it is primarily Berkhof who emphasizes the necessity of having an ordered, rather than disordered, society in which to live, and that the Church plays a part in this order.

The doctrine of Common Grace is a recognition that, in addition to the blessings of the Christian life, there are blessings given to all people, that in the regular course of life there are "many traces of the true, the good, and the beautiful." It seeks to explain how there is order in the world when the whole world is under the curse of sin, how the earth provides abundance to both the saved and the unsaved, and how sinful people continue to have a knowledge of God and of the difference between good and evil. [20]

As Berkhof states: "This is a grace which is communal, does not pardon nor purify human nature, and does not affect the salvation of sinners. It curbs the destructive power of sin, maintains in a measure the moral order of the universe, thus making an orderly life possible, distributes in varying degrees gifts and talents among men, promotes the development of science and art, and showers untold blessings upon the children of men."[21]

Common Grace may refer to the Holy Spirit's work of exerting moral influence on all people so that "sin is restrained, order is maintained in social life, and civil righteousness is

---
20 Berkhof, p. 432.
21 Berkhof, p. 434.

promoted;" or it may refer to blessings given to all men, such as sunshine and rain, and food, clothing and shelter. In addition, it serves to develop the talents of all people in order that they may more and more exercise dominion over the physical world. [22]

According to Berkhof, Common Grace works through many means, of which the following are most important:

"1. THE LIGHT OF GOD'S REVELATION.
This is fundamental for…it serves to guide the conscience of the natural man. Paul speaks of the Gentiles who do by nature the things of the law, 'in that they show the word of the law written in their hearts, their conscience bearing witness therewith, and their thoughts one with another accusing or else excusing them.' Rom. 2:14,15. Calvin in commenting on this passage says that such Gentiles 'prove that there is imprinted on their hearts a discrimination and judgment by which they distinguish between what is just and unjust, between what is honest and dishonest.'[*Comm. on Romans in loco.*]

"2. GOVERNMENTS.
Of these too it may be said that they are at once the fruit and the means of common grace. According to Rom. 13, governments are ordained of God, to maintain good order in society. To resist them is to resist the ordinance of God. The ruler, says Paul, 'is a minister of God to thee for good.' Rom. 13:4.

---
22   Berkhof, p. 442.

"3. PUBLIC OPINION.

The natural light that shines in the hearts of men, especially when re-enforced by the influence of God's special revelation, results in the forming of a public opinion that is in external conformity with the law of God; and this has a tremendous influence on the conduct of men who are very sensitive to the judgment of public opinion. Naturally public opinion will be a means of common grace only when it is formed under the influence of God's revelation. If it is not controlled by conscience, acting in harmony with the light of nature, or by the Word of God, it becomes a mighty influence for evil.

"4. DIVINE PUNISHMENTS AND REWARDS.

As God allows the consequences of sin to affect people in this life, and rewards deeds that conform to the divine law, evil is restrained in the world. 'By these means, whatever there is of moral goodness in the world is greatly encouraged. Many shun evil and seek that which is good, not because they fear the Lord, but because they feel that good brings its own reward and best serves their interests.'"

The fruits of Common Grace are many, and only a few will be discussed here:

"1. THE RESTRAINT OF SIN.

Through the operation of common grace sin is restrained in the lives of individuals and in society. The element of corruption that entered the life of the human race is not permitted, for the present, to accomplish its disintegrating work.

"2. THE PRESERVATION OF SOME SENSE OF TRUTH, MORALITY AND RELIGION.

It is due to common grace that man still retains some sense of the true, the good, and the beautiful, often appreciates these to a rather surprising degree, and reveals a desire for truth, for external morality, and even for certain forms of religion. Paul speaks of Gentiles who 'show the work of the law written in their hearts, their conscience bearing witness therewith, and their thoughts one with another accusing or else excusing them,' Rom. 2:15, and even says of those who gave free vent to their wicked lives that they knew the truth of God, though they hindered the truth in unrighteousness and exchanged it for a lie. (Rom. 1:18-20)

"3. THE PERFORMANCE OF OUTWARD GOOD AND CIVIL RIGHTEOUSNESS.

Common grace enables man to perform … that which is right in civil or natural affairs, … natural good works especially in social relations, works that are outwardly and objectively in harmony with the law of God, though entirely destitute of any spiritual quality.

"4. MANY NATURAL BLESSINGS.

To common grace man further owes all the natural blessings which he receives in the present life. Though he has forfeited all the blessings of God, he receives abundant tokens of the goodness of God from day to day. There are several passages of Scripture from which it appears abundantly that God showers many of His good gifts on all men indiscriminately, that is, upon the good and the bad, the elect and the reprobate, such as: Gen. 17:20 (comp. vs. 18); 39:5; Ps. 145:9,15,16; Matt. 5:44,45; Luke 6:35,36; Acts 14:16,17; I Tim. 4:10. And these gifts are intended as blessings, not only for the good but also for the evil." [23]

Without Common Grace, our society would be chaotic and fully under the power of sin in all of its manifestations. It is through a society's adherence to the Moral Law of God that Common Grace can be most effective; in fact, without adherence to the Moral Law, that grace cannot be restrained and sin allowed to flourish. This is what we see happening in the 21st century.

Consider Berkhof's statement about Public Opinion: "Naturally public opinion will be a means of common grace only when it is formed under the influence of God's revelation. If it is not controlled by conscience, acting in harmony with the light of nature, or by the Word of God, it becomes a mighty influence for evil." Public opinion, when not informed by the Moral Law of God, is a force for great evil. When people begin to "call evil good and good evil" (Isaiah 5:20), we will see less and less good and more and more evil.

The only answer to this is for the Church to speak out against the mis-interpretations of the Moral Law. The Church, preaching the whole counsel of God, is the only source for people to hear the truth. By refusing to confront public opinion, the Church allows evil to flourish. By its silence, the

---
[23] Berkhof, pp. 432-446

Church hides the truth of God from those who need to hear it. As Paul writes: "How are they to hear without someone preaching?" (Romans 10:14)

CHAPTER 10

PHARISEES THEN AND NOW

For a great many people, it is very hard to connect biblical and historical events with what we are experiencing today. There are many people in the church who see the Pharisees as merely religious leaders. With this understanding, they wrongly assume that Jesus had nothing to say to the political leaders of His day.

However, when Jesus spoke to the Pharisees, he was in fact speaking to the political leaders of His day. Of course, the ultimate political authority rested with the Roman Empire and its representatives, but that does not negate the political influence of the Pharisees of Israel. Historically and biblically, the Pharisees of Jesus' day were both political and spiritual leaders. The Pharisees came to power "during the period of independence that followed the revolt [of the

Maccabees, 167-160 B.C.], [and] some of the Greek rulers who controlled Palestine favored the Pharisaic party. As a result of this favoritism, Pharisees came to be represented on the Sanhedrin (the highest ruling body and court of justice among the Jewish people in the time of Jesus).[24] *The Illustrated Bible Dictionary* defines Pharisees as "a religious and political party in Palestine in New Testament times."[25]

According to Jacob Neusner, "The Pharisees constituted a political party which sought, and for a time evidently won, domination of the political institutions of the Maccabean kingdom. In other words, however they might hope to *teach* people to conform to the Torah, they were prepared to coerce them to conform through the instruments of government."[26]

The political power of the Pharisees was great, and Jesus' choice to confront them carried no small consequences, as we can see through Scripture. As Joachim Jeremias explains: "[those with] the motive to follow Jesus among those who 'travailed and were 'heavy laden', were the 'publicans' and 'sinners'. But as a whole, the people looked to the Pharisees ... as models of piety, and as embodiments of the ideal life which the scribes, these men of divine and secret knowledge, had set before them. It was an act of unparalleled risk which Jesus performed when, from the full power of his consciousness of sovereignty, he openly and fearlessly called these men to repentance, and this act brought him to the cross."[27]

---

24   Jeremias, 262
25   Lockyear, p. 830.
26   Neusner, p. 49.
27   Jeremias, p. 267.

Biblically, we can see in Scripture that the Pharisees acted as "government leaders" when they sent officers to attempt to arrest Jesus (John 7:32), when they listened as officers reported that they will not arrest Jesus (John 7:45), when they conferred about not arresting Jesus (John 11:47), when they sent officers to arrest Jesus (John 18:3), and when they delivered Jesus to Pilate to be crucified (John 18:28).

Jesus' anger at the Pharisees, in my opinion, was due not so much to unbelief and misuse of power; rather it was due to their support for the "tradition of the elders," or interpretation of the law by the Scribes. In other words, the Pharisees and the Scribes were guilty of adding to and misrepresenting the Law of God. More than anyone else, they should have known better. It was more than an individual sin. It was corporate sin. They were the **caretakers of the law** leading a whole nation away from the very God who would weep over their loss.

So, who is adding to and misrepresenting the Law of God today? In other words, who are the present day "Pharisees"? The obvious answer is our political leaders. For example, God says to love our neighbor. In the minds of many, love means that we must allow a person to do whatever he or she chooses to do. So, if a woman does not want to be pregnant, and wants to kill her unborn child, their concept of love dictates that it must be her right to do so.

In I Corinthians 10:32 we read, "Give no offense to Jews or to Greeks or to the church of God." In the minds of many today, giving offense has become an unpardonable sin. Any "offensive" speech, meaning basically any speech that any other person does not like, is considered "hate speech" and should be banned. Of course, there is offensive speech, and we are to be careful in what we say; but in our culture today, speaking of the Gospel or the Law of God has become "hate speech."

Consider the promise made by Christ: "I came that they may have life and have it abundantly." (John 10:10) What does abundant life mean? Having whatever we want? Doing whatever we please? Should the Church cover over the sins of its people in order to allow them to live the "abundant life" that they believe they were meant to live?

As followers of Christ today, do we get this? Are church leaders ready to say to the State, or any other corporate group who controls the mechanisms of society, "if you misrepresent God's Moral Law" there will be a heavy price to pay—and that means all of us? Also, are you contrite enough so that you are willing to imitate Jesus' **style** as well as **substance**? Some people have responded, "Well, we're not Jesus." Think about what Paul said in 1 Cor. 1:11: "Imitate me as I imitate Christ." The meaning here is very clear. We are to show boldness, and sometimes righteous anger, as Jesus did in the Temple, especially when the meaning of the Moral Law and the believers who follow it are under attack. Esther did, and she saved her people from annihilation.

CHAPTER 11

CHRISTIANS AND POLITICS

Is any of this political? Of course it is. And, as Christian citizens, we have a choice to make: to despise politics or to see it as a discipline ordained of God. Its purposes will be either for good or evil. There is no in-between. But Christians are called to be "salt and light" in all areas of life. Below are some important points to remember about political science that may not have been covered in a college classroom, but are never-the-less important to remember:

1. Much of what goes on in politics is about compromise, but certainly not moral compromise. As in every other discipline where people are working together, having your own way on every issue is impossible. There must be a compromise which is moral. Bottom line, you must agree to work it out.

Sometimes, though, the situation which is before voters is what we call "moral equivalence." Simply put, there are some things which are far worse than others, so we must make a choice--or choose not to vote--between what we used to call "the lesser of two evils."

Think of Rahab, if you will. Scripture says the spies entered the house of a prostitute, so most readers would assume that at this time Rahab was still a prostitute. Obviously, at some point in the future, she no longer practiced the "world's oldest profession." Now, for some, an overnight stay at Rahab's place might present a dilemma. Just let that sink in for a moment. The spies had a choice—either spend the night in the home of a prostitute, thus becoming "unclean" or spend the night in open view on the streets, but remaining "clean." The "lesser of two evils" dictated that they choose to stay with Rahab. We are not given all the details, but we do know that this was part of God's plan to deliver Israel.

Now, fast forward to the more recent past. In most of the recent presidential elections in the United States, there has been no clear moral leader. Both of the major candidates have been flawed, with blatant sins in their past. Because of this, we must look beyond the candidates themselves to the party platforms they have pledged to support. We should look for things like a commitment to protect unborn and born-alive children; to protect the Church from interference by the State; to protect our citizens from violence; etc. For most Evangelical voters it should boil down to "which is worse," or "no moral equivalence," between a political party that agrees to support these things and one that actually promises to work against them.

2. There is no doubt about it, "politics is dirty business," but does that mean we have nothing whatsoever to do with it? A fellow pastor in 2016 said to me as I made my "moral equivalent" argument: "Charlie, I'm ashamed to be a Christian, and think I'll just stay home on election day." I responded: "Well, I'm not ashamed to be a Christian, but I'd like to tell you about a scene in the movie "Walk the Line" that may change your mind. Maybelle and June Carter talked on the bank overlooking the river as they watched Johnny Cash try to get his tractor unstuck after driving it into the river mud:

> **Maybelle Carter:** "You should go down there to him, June."
> **June:** "Mama"
> **Maybelle:** "He's all mixed up."
> **June:** "I'm not going down there. If I go down there…"
> **Maybelle:** "You already are down there, honey."[28]

We are all already "down there" when it comes to politics. Whatever happens politically will affect all of us. To choose not to vote is to choose to allow greater opportunity for evil to win the day.

Jerry Newcombe has given us ten reasons why the Church should not abandon politics:

---
28   Walk the Line, n.p.

1. The Word of God has something to say about all of life, beyond just the spiritual.

2. Bible itself addresses the issue of governing in different texts.

3. The Scriptures also teach that on occasion, there may be a need for civil disobedience.

4. Nature abhors a vacuum. Someone will be involved in politics. Why not us?

5. When the Church does not speak out, evil can fill that void.

6. The Church is called to be salt and light. Salt preserves and prevents decay.

7. We pray, "Thy kingdom come, Thy will be done, on earth as it is in heaven."

8. Christians bless everybody when we properly apply our faith to politics.

9. Politics may be the calling of some in the congregation. Therefore, ministers should encourage political involvement that is motivated by the desire to serve.

10. Religion and morality are "indispensable supports to our political prosperity."[29]

The full text of Newcombe's article can be found in the Appendix to this book.

---

[29] Newcome, n.p.

CHAPTER 12

SILENCE AND LUKEWARMNESS

For centuries, the Church has wrestled with the issues of when to speak, how much to speak, or whether to speak at all, about violations of the Moral Law by the State. Reasons for this differ, but clearly fear and ignorance on the part of the Church is foremost. Nevertheless, when the State legislates immorality and encourages others to commit the same sin, this is different. Why? Because God has always held His people accountable to flee sin personally and to stand boldly against it. Furthermore, a Christian church could not possibly honor God if it says nothing concerning the State's violations of any of God's Commandments.

Respect and honor of God's Moral Law never changes, even if governments and politicians change. And "how will they [those today who legislate immorality and those who follow their lead] hear without a preacher?" Apart from the Bible, which it is the sacred duty of the Christian Church to teach, the Moral Law and its prophetic warning cannot be understood, nor will it bring conviction. This was true during slavery, during Civil Rights & racial reconciliation, and is still true today when lawmakers flagrantly, and without fear of recourse, continue to violate God's Moral Law by supporting abortion, re-defining biblical marriage & gender, bearing false witness, and many other notorious sins. Do we dare to call this sin on the part of the State notorious? Do we dare to call the church's silence sinful? If we don't, then we are saying that the State's violations of God's Moral Code are acceptable.

Let's be honest, the Church has been dead wrong about the need and command to speak out about violations of the Moral Law by the State. Therefore, consider these following truths that should be taught by every Christian pastor and Church:

1. There never was a wall of separation between Church & State, either constitutionally or biblically. It is unfortunate that "separation of church and state" passes as an axiom (or "self-evident truth"), because the original intent (a letter by Thomas Jefferson to the Danbury Baptist Church) was not a matter of separation, rather a matter of church protection from a state religion.

2. It is not the prerogative of the State or Church to prohibit, discourage, or intimidate any person or group

from addressing violations of the Moral Law of God by the State. In fact, the Church especially should encourage it.

3. The Church must recognize the importance of the Moral Law in bestowing the benefits of Common Grace. Although distinct from Saving Grace, Common Grace allows us all to live in an orderly, relatively peaceful society. As Jesus said "[God] causes His sun to rise on the evil and the good, and sends rain on the righteous and the unrighteous." (Matt. 5:45). Berkhof, in his Systematic Theology, explains that "[Common grace] curbs the destructive power of sin, maintains in a measure the moral order of the universe, thus making an orderly life possible, distributes in varying degrees gifts and talents among men, promotes the development of science and art, and showers untold blessings upon the children of men."[30]

If the Church neglects to defend the Moral Law and refuses to confront the State when it flagrantly violates it or redefines it, the blessings of Common Grace become more problematic. How can a government allow its people to live in a society in which the "power of sin is curbed" and the "moral order of the universe is maintained" when it encourages sin and rejects that moral order? Should the Church merely wring its corporate hands and cry, "Woe is me!" or should the Church speak out to right the wrongs perpetrated by the State?

---

[30]   Berkhof

4. Silence in the face of evil is unacceptable to God. We are commanded to speak out against evil, as illustrated in the following Scripture passages:

> **Ezekiel 33:6** - "If the watchman . . . does not warn the people . . . I will hold the watchman accountable for his blood."
>
> **Ephesians 5:11** - "Do not participate in the unfruitful deeds of darkness, but rather expose them."
>
> **Proverbs 31:8-9** - "Speak up for those who have no voice, for the justice of all who are dispossessed. Speak up, judge righteously, and defend the cause of the oppressed and needy."
>
> **Proverbs 32:3** - "For when I kept silent, my bones wasted away through my groaning all day long."

Neither is lukewarmness acceptable to God. We are to serve God and Him only and to love Him with all our heart, with all our soul, and with all our might. (Deut. 6:5)

> **Revelation 3:13-16**- "And to the angel of the church in Laodicea write: The words of the Amen, the faithful and true witness, the beginning of God's creation. I know your works: you are neither cold nor hot. Would that you were either cold or hot! So, because you are lukewarm, and neither hot nor cold, I will spit you out of my mouth."

Titus 1:16 - "They profess to know God, but they deny him by their works. They are detestable, disobedient, unfit for any good work."

Matthew 6:24 - "No one can serve two masters, for either he will hate the one and love the other, or he will be devoted to the one and despise the other.

Luke 6:46,47 - "Why do you call me, 'Lord, Lord,' and do not do what I say? As for everyone who comes to me and hears my words and puts them into practice, I will show you what they are like. They are like a man building a house, who dug down deep and laid the foundation on rock."

Finally, every pastor and church should consider the commentary written by Dr. R. C. Sproul concerning passages from Joshua 1 and 5, in which he emphasizes courage, confidence, faithfulness, and victory:

1. God's speech to Joshua on the border of Canaan is filled with exhortations for Joshua to be strong and courageous.
2. If Joshua embodied any godly trait, it was courage.
3. Joshua was confident that the Israelites could take the land.
4. We must note that the courage Joshua is encouraged to have is not exclusively military courage.

5. Joshua's military success would not be determined by his plans; rather, His faithfulness to the Word of God would be the key to taking Canaan successfully.

6. If he lacked courage to lead the people in obedience, they would not complete their task.

7. Joshua recognized that The Commander of the Lord's Army and pre-incarnate Christ was no ordinary individual, that He could be either a powerful ally or strong enemy. This commander revealed that He was on Joshua's side—or more appropriately, that Joshua should be on His side. If we are on God's side, the victory is ours.[31]

If the Commander of the Lord's Army, Jesus Christ, gave His blessing and military success to Joshua, then He will also give his blessing to the Church which Our Lord established. In turn, the Church should also give its blessing to its leaders and members who fight for the truth of God.

If the Church which Our Lord established was wrong in the past about "separation of church and state" by adopting a wrong "spirituality" doctrine, thus causing great harm and confusion over the centuries, then it must reject and discontinue this teaching altogether.

If the Church which Our Lord established, and over which He is still King, has unknowingly confused social issues with clearly biblical-moral issues, and therefore thinks itself

---
[31] Sproul, n.p.

SILENCE AND LUKEWARMNESS

justified in its silence, it must do so no longer and speak directly and boldly about violations of the Moral Law. There is no alternative. That is the biblical standard.

If the Church which Our Lord established does not heed the warnings of Scripture concerning its silence and lukewarmness, then it must be prepared to pay a terrible price.

There is a pattern here, and it is one of non-involvement because the Church thinks it has better things to do, things which it deems "more spiritual." It would prefer to let the State handle its own business, even if that business is the overthrow of God's Moral Law. It would prefer to be silent in the face of evil. This must change if the Church expects to be on the side of the Lord.

These and other related topics are critical for the Church to teach and emphasize, especially to young people, so that they "may be thoroughly equipped for every good work" (2 Timothy 3:17). Although there is much work to be done in our nation's capital among legislators, where many denominations are at work, there is a much greater work to be done in the local church and connected ministries.

In both areas the Christian Church must be the leader with these words: "In matters of morality, the Christian Church should navigate the ship of state."

CHAPTER 13

ACCURATELY HANDLE THE WORD OF TRUTH

We are not all academic theologians, but as Christians we are charged with doing our best "to present ourselves to God as one approved, a worker who has no need to be ashamed, rightly handling the word of truth" (2 Tim. 2:15,).

Apply this Biblical teaching and logic, if you will, to church and state issues. If something is a moral [and therefore spiritual] issue, then I think it is reasonable to conclude that the Church must speak up in order to protect that which is spiritual. Very specifically, and with Spiritual power, the Church must say to the State "you do not have the moral authority to usurp the Moral Law by redefining what is sinful and what is not."

Let me illustrate just how powerful a statement that would be if spoken from the pulpit. Let's suppose that a "good" Southern Baptist politician and a "good" Roman Catholic politician attend church one Sunday, and the pastor and priest stop in the middle of their sermons, look directly at each politician and say this: "There are over 68 million Catholics and 16 million Southern Baptists in America. By next Sunday all of the leadership of our congregations will have signed a letter to members of Congress and the other two branches of government with this brief statement: *No branch of government has the moral authority to overturn the Moral Law of God. Along with the leaders of other denominations, as Christians, we will present a united front to oppose such actions whenever they occur.*

You might think this is unloving. After all, "God so loved the world." What right do some church leaders have to dictate the Moral Law for everyone? If God loves the whole world, then who is to say what is right and wrong for every individual?

Dr. John Tweeddale presents a powerful answer to this age-old question:

> "One of the most surprising twists of John 3:16 is that we are told God loves the world. We might be tempted to think that there is much about the world for God to love... The world we know is filled with texture, intrigue, opportunity, and cheer. The problem is that for all that is good and interesting and beautiful about

the world, it is overrun with sinners. ...No matter how wonderful the world may appear, it is not worthy of God's redeeming love.

"Understanding how undeserving the world is of God's love is the key to John 3:16. Only then will we appreciate the unexpected gift that God gives. This point was well made many years ago by the esteemed theologian Benjamin Breckinridge Warfield. In his sermon "God's Immeasurable Love," Warfield probes the meaning of the term "world" (Greek kosmos) in John 3:16 in order to plumb the depths of God's love.

"What is the meaning of "world" in this passage? Drawing from the insights of Warfield, there are four possible answers.

"In the first place, many people believe that "world" means all people without exception. In other words, when John 3:16 says that God loves the world, it means that He loves every person, head for head, equally... Yet this viewpoint contradicts the Bible's teaching on God's judgment as is evidenced by the immediate context in John 3:17–21.

"Second, others argue that "world" means all people without distinction. This option emphasizes that God loves more than one type of person or ethnic group... While this view has the benefit of being undoubtedly right... it doesn't quite capture the jolting contrast between "God so loved" and "the world" that John 3:16 deliberately draws.

"Third, a popular nuance of the previous option among Reformed theologians is to argue that "world" in John 3:16 refers to the elect... Again, this view strikes an important note by underscoring the biblical doctrine of election, but the focus of the term "world" in John 3:16 is not so much on the identity of God's people but on the nature of God's love.

"This leads us to the final option. A solid case can be made for believing that "world" refers to the quality of God's love. Warfield convincingly states:

"'[World] is not here a term of extension so much as a term of intensity... [It does not suggest] that the world is so big that it takes a great deal of love to embrace it all, but that the world is so bad that it takes a great kind of love to love it at all.'

"The world represents sinful humanity and is not worthy of God's saving love. Apart from the love of God, the world stands under God's condemnation. But in Christ, believers experience God's surprising, redeeming, and never-ending love. John 3:16 is not about the greatness of the world but about the greatness of God.[32]

---

[32] Tweeddale, p. 5

CHAPTER 14

NEVER TAKE A BACK SEAT

Christians should always be in the driver's seat apologetically. That should be our strong point. Be nice to the opposition, but do not let them get away with misusing Scripture. And, if you are not sure of the meaning of Scripture, then go home and look it up or call someone you trust. Do your homework!

Too often, Christians are unprepared to counter the cultural and political beliefs of others. We know that what they are saying is wrong, but we are not sure why. Or perhaps we are sure why, but we are afraid of confrontation.

If we are to be salt and light, then we must give our fears to God and speak boldly about the Law of God. If we refuse to speak, how will others hear? Perhaps you will be uncomfortable. Perhaps you will be ridiculed. That is to be expected. Be prepared for it. Embrace it. As Christ said, "Blessed are those who are persecuted for righteousness' sake, for theirs is the kingdom of heaven. Blessed are you when others revile you and persecute you and utter all kinds of evil against you falsely on my account. Rejoice and be glad, for your reward is great in heaven, for so they persecuted the prophets who were before you." (Matthew 5:10-12)

Below is a discussion of some of the major moral issues of the present day.

1. ABORTION

The general argument against abortion is that it is murder. Those who want to allow abortion argue that it is not murder because the baby cannot live on its own outside the mother's body. This argument seems to infer that the baby is not "alive" until it is actually born.

Therefore, we must ask how we know whether someone is alive. I would contend that if someone is not proved to be dead, the presumption is that the person is alive. So let us look at the definition of death according to the World Health Organization: [Death is determined by] "Loss of Capacity for Consciousness: Lack of current or any future potential for awareness, wakefulness, interaction, and capacity for sensory perception of, or responsiveness to the external environment. Emphasis was placed on the predominance of brain function for determination of death. Death is a single phenomenon based on cessation of brain function (loss of capacity of consciousness and brainstem reflexes) with two mechanisms to reach that point: (i) permanent absence of circulation or (ii) subsequent to a catastrophic brain injury."[33]

If this is how death is determined, it would logically follow that the opposite of the condition described above would indicate life. Presence of Capacity for Consciousness, presence of current or future potential for awareness, etc., continuation of brain function, brainstem reflexes, and circulation should indicate that a person is alive.

Now that we have established a working definition of life, let us compare that definition to a description of a developing fetus/child. In the first month after conception, blood cells are taking shape, and circulation will begin. The tiny "heart" tube will beat 65 times a minute by the end of the fourth week.[34]

In the second month of development, the neural tube (brain, spinal cord and other neural tissue of the central nervous system) is well formed. By week 12 of the third month, the baby's arms, hands, fingers, feet and toes are fully formed. At this stage, the baby is starting to explore a bit by doing things like opening and closing its fists and mouth. By the end of the third month, the baby is fully formed. [35]

It seems obvious from the evidence that an unborn child exhibits life since its brain, brainstem, and circulatory

---

33   International Guidelines, p. 32
34   Fetal Development, n.p.
35   Fetal Development, n.p.

system is working. Also, the definition of life which we have developed states that there must be the <u>potential for future awareness, wakefulness, interaction, and capacity for sensory perception of, or responsiveness to the external environment</u>. The person does not have to exhibit those things in his/her present context; he or she merely must have the <u>potential</u> for such things in the future. Clearly an unborn child would have such potential. In fact, we do not even need to discuss potential, because by the twelfth week, the baby is actually beginning to interact with its environment.

So it would seem obvious that an unborn child is alive. Which leads to the further question, is the killing of this living person murder?

The definition of murder, according to the US Code, is the unlawful killing of a human being perpetrated from a premeditated design unlawfully and maliciously to effect the death of any human being.[36] The problem lies with the term "unlawfully." At the present time, abortion is lawful, because the government has usurped the right to define the Moral Law and declared it to be so. But it is still murder in God's eyes.

We could also consider abortion to be child abuse, which means "intentionally or knowingly causing death or serious bodily injury to a child."[37]

---

36 18 U.S. Code § 1111, n.p.
37 18 U.S. Code § 1111, n.p.

God has said the following about unborn children:

> **Jeremiah 1:5** - Before I formed you in the womb I knew you, and before you were born I consecrated you.
>
> **Luke 1:41, 44** - And it came to pass, that when Elizabeth heard the salutation of Mary, the infant leaped in her womb… for joy.
>
> **Psalm 139:13, 15** - For you formed my inward parts; you knitted me together in my mother's womb…. My frame was not hidden from you, when I was being made in secret, intricately woven in the depths of the earth.
>
> **Exodus 21:22** - When men strive together and hit a pregnant woman, so that her children come out, but there is no harm [to the woman], the one who hit her shall surely be fined, as the woman's husband shall impose on him, and he shall pay as the judges determine.

2. GENDER

The number of genders that exist and the ability to change one's gender are hot topics of discussion as I am writing today. The argument is that we are assigned a gender at birth and that we should be able to choose our own gender and change that gender as we may desire.

The basic question here is the number of possible genders that exist. We need to back to high school biology to answer this question. According to scientists Laura Hake and Clare

O'Conner, "Normally, cells from females contain two X chromosomes and cells from males contain an X and a Y chromosome. Occasionally, individuals are born with [an abnormal number of sex chromosomes], and the sex of these individuals is always determined by the absence or presence of a Y chromosome."[38]

People are not "assigned" a gender at birth. We may be assigned topics for term papers or jobs to do at work, but we are not "assigned" our gender. The presence or absence of a Y chromosome will produce very distinct physical characteristics. The doctor does need to tell the baby's parents what the baby's gender is. They can pretty much tell that on their own.

From this, we know that there are two scientific as well as biblical genders. "Male and female He created them." (Genesis 1:27) A person may choose to dress as a different gender, or even to have surgery to appear to be the opposite gender, but if a medical examiner were to test the DNA of an unknown individual, even a skeleton, that examiner would be able to tell whether this person were a man or a woman. His or her lifestyle would not be reflected in the DNA.

A Christian lady (I guess) asked me if I thought there were more than two genders. I responded, "No, there are not. Science supports this and so does the Bible." She responded, "Pastor, are you sure?" I said, "I am absolutely certain." My question to the Church is this: "If indeed, this lady is a Christian, what can

---

[38]   Hake and O'Connor, n.p.

the Church do differently to make sure that these "self-evident" truths and unbiblical teachings are addressed?

So basically, there are two genders, but people may choose to live a lifestyle that rejects biological gender. How does God feel about that?

> **Deuteronomy 22:5** - A woman shall not wear a man's garment, nor shall a man put on a woman's cloak, for whoever does these things is an abomination to the Lord your God. [This verse may seem harsh to us today, and we are not advocating that anyone treat such a person harshly. But this is God's opinion on this matter.]
>
> **Leviticus 18:22** - You shall not lie with a male as with a woman; it is an abomination.
>
> **Leviticus 20:13** -If a man lies with a male as with a woman, both of them have committed an abomination; they shall surely be put to death; their blood is upon them.
>
> **I Corinthians 6:9-10** - Or do you not know that the unrighteous will not inherit the kingdom of God? Do not be deceived: neither the sexually immoral, nor idolaters, not adulterers, not men who practice homosexuality, nor thieves, nor the greedy, nor drunkards, nor revilers, nor swindlers will inherit the kingdom of God. [Note that homosexuality is one of many sins on this list. All are equally serious.]

I Timothy 1:8-10 - Now we know that the law is good, if one uses it lawfully, understanding this, that the law is not laid down for the just but for the lawless and disobedient, for the ungodly and sinners, for the unholy and profane, for those who strike their fathers and mothers, for murderers, the sexually immoral, men who practice homosexuality, enslavers, liars, perjurers, and whatever else is contrary to sound doctrine.

Romans 1:18-19, 21-22, 26-27 - For the wrath of God is revealed from heaven against all ungodliness and unrighteousness of men, who by their unrighteousness suppress the truth. For what can be known about God is plain to them, because God has shown it to them... So they are without excuse. For although they knew God, they did not honor him as God or give thanks to him, but they became futile in their thinking, and their foolish hearts were darkened. Claiming to be wise, they became fools... For this reason God gave them up to dishonorable passions. For their women exchanged natural relations for those that are contrary to nature; and the men likewise gave up natural relations with women and were consumed with passion for one another, men committing shameless acts with men and receiving in themselves the due penalty for their error.

3. MARRIAGE

The question of gender almost always accompanies a discussion about marriage. How does God feel about marriage between two men or two women?

The answer to the question about marriage between two men or two women can be found in the discussion of gender above, especially the passage in Romans 1.

Here are other verses which refer to marriage. In every Bible reference to marriage, the Scripture refers to a husband and a wife. There are no Scripture verses which refer to husband and husband or to wife and wife. Two people of the same gender may declare their love and loyalty to one another, but this is not marriage in the eyes of God.

> **Genesis 2:24** - Therefore a man shall leave his father and his mother and hold fast to his wife, and they shall become one flesh. (This verse is quoted many times in other books of the Bible.)
>
> **Matthew 19:4-5** - [Jesus said} Have you not read that he who created them from the beginning made them male and female, and said, "Therefore a man shall leave his father and his mother and hold fast to his wife, and they shall become one flesh."
>
> **Deuteronomy 24:5** - When a man is newly married, he shall not go out with the army or be liable for any other public duty. He shall be free at home one year to be happy with his wife whom he has taken.
>
> **I Corinthians 7:2-3** - But because of the temptation to sexual immorality, each man should have his own wife and each woman her own husband. The husband

should give to his wife her conjugal rights, and likewise the wife to her husband.

4. BEARING FALSE WITNESS

The Ninth Commandment states: "You shall not bear false witness against your neighbor." (Exodus 20:16) Many people assume that this commandment refers to lying in general, but it is most directly concerned about witnesses in criminal cases. James Anderson explains that in Hebrew law, if a witness was found to be a "false witness," he would be given the same penalty that would have been given to the accused, up to and including the death penalty. In order for justice to prevail, the courts must hear the truth. The accused deserves for the truth to be told, whether it convicts or exonerates him.[39]

Of course, the rest of Scripture makes it clear that God requires us to tell the truth in other circumstances, not only in court situations.

In recent years, we have seen a proliferation of people bearing false witness in Congress, in court, and in the court of public opinion. Many innocent people have had their lives ruined by the lies of others. Some have spent thousands of dollars to defend themselves against false accusations. The media have also participated in spreading false information about those in the news, so that it becomes almost impossible to separate the truth from lies.

---

[39] Anderson, n.p.

Such lies are violations of the Ninth Commandment and also violate the injunctions to treat others as we would want to be treated and to love our enemies. If we love only those who love us, Jesus says we are no better than the tax collectors. (Matthew 5:46) The problem seems to have been an issue with the tax collectors (i.e., the government) all along.

5. CLIMATE CHANGE

Although this probably does not qualify as a "Moral issue," many Christians have prioritized the environment to the point of acquiescing on many violations of God's laws. We would agree with them that it is important to care for the earth we live on. God instructed Adam and Eve to tend the Garden and to care for the animals.

However, Christians should also remember that this is not our ultimate home, and that God will create a new earth for us to live in forever. In that new earth, there will be no sin, no destruction, no decay, and probably no "climate change."

We should also be cautious about believing politicians or scientists who warn us that the earth can last only another ten years, or fifty years, or one hundred years, etc. We must remember that the earth will last as long as God has determined that it should last, and He alone knows when the end will come. (Matthew 24:36)

6. CRITICAL THEORY

Critical Theory, including Critical Race Theory, is not a single issue, but rather a worldview that is influencing much of the discussion of moral issues in our culture today. The next chapter will give a brief overview of Critical Theory and how it relates to the Christian worldview.

CHAPTER 15

CRITICAL THEORY

We readily admit to not being experts on Critical Theory, but we have researched the issue and felt that it must be included in this book.

A BRIEF GLIMPSE INTO CRITICAL THEORY

Critical Race Theory (CRT) is a popular perspective on race that is quickly gaining momentum, although most people who have been influenced by this theory are probably not aware of its existence or are only marginally aware. CRT is a sub-category of Critical Theory, which deals with multiple minority distinctions. Originally based on Marxist ideology, this theory uses many identity markers—race, class, sex, sexual orientation, gender identity, physical ability, age, weight, etc.—to divide the world into two categories: the oppressed and the oppressors. The goal of those who work in this area is to free the oppressed from bondage, whether it be physical, economic, cultural, or moral.[40]

Those who remember the Feminist movement will remember that it was an attempt to free women from disparities that existed between women and men, such as income disparities, healthcare disparities, childcare disparities, etc. Today, Feminism could be classified as Critical Feminist Theory. However, Critical Theory delves much deeper than obvious disparities. Critical Theory asserts that oppression is systemic and has infiltrated all aspects of life.

Critical <u>Race</u> Theory specifically deals with those who are oppressed due to their race. Some of the disparities between races are readily apparent; for example, "white people on the whole have more wealth than people of color, white people tend to make more money than people of color, and white people are more likely to have health insurance than people of color."[41] But again, Critical Theory, in this case Critical RACE Theory, teaches that everything is viewed through the lens of race, so much so that oppressors (in this case, white people) are not even aware that their thoughts and/or actions are racist. The only way to change the situation for the oppressed is to dismantle the present system and institute a new one.

Critical Theory argues that the basic evil in society today is "hegemonic power," the ability of a particular group to impose its norms, values and expectations on the rest of

---

40 Shenvi and Sawyer, p. 2.
41 Otten, n.p.

society. "In any relationship between groups that define one another (men/women, able-bodied/disabled, young/old), the dominant group is the group that is valued more highly, and that group sets the norms by which the minoritized group is judged....A member of the dominant group benefits from—and is morally tainted by—the privilege he obtains from his group membership."[42]

For example, in Critical Theory, men are a dominant group who impose their norms and values on others, making women an oppressed group. Critical theorists would seek to liberate women not only from physical oppression (violence, income inequality, sexual harassment, etc.), they would also want to free them from male norms such as traditional gender roles in marriage or the workplace.[43]

In Critical Race Theory, racism is not defined as actions which favor one race over another or which physically or mentally demean a person of another race. Rather, it is the system that has been developed by white men to impose their values and norms on people of other ethnicities.[44]

Therefore, all white men are inherently guilty of racism because they are a part of the dominant group labeled "white men," even if they have never even thought a negative thought about another race. According to critical theorists, the concept of race itself is a social construct made up by the dominant classes.

---

42 Shenvi, p. 4.
43 Shenvi, p. 7.
44 Otten, n.p.

Critical Theory also asserts that the "lived experience" of oppression gives the oppressed access to truths that are generally not known to oppressors. This is multiplied by the concept of "Intersectionality," which means that a person can be a member of many oppressed groups. All of those groups will contribute to that person's "lived experience."[45]

For example, a white gay male who is left-handed is a member of the dominant groups of white and male, but he is also a member of the oppressed groups of gay and left-handed. A white woman with a disability is a member of the dominant group white, but also of the oppressed groups women and disabled.

Critical Theory insists that dominant groups must defer to the claims of oppressed groups. "Demands for objective evidence and rational dialogue are seen as invalidating the oppressed person's "lived experience." In fact, those demands illustrate white male norms which have been imposed on others.[46]

WHERE CHRISTIANS AND CRITICAL THEORISTS CAN AGREE

As Christians, we do not disagree with every aspect of Critical Theory. First, we can agree that the concept of race is a social construct and not a biological fact. People may have different physical characteristics, but we are all members of the "human" race. In fact, the Bible does not use the word "race" as a biological classification of people.

---
45   Shenvi, p. 8.
46   Shenvi, p. 9.

When it is used, the term refers to a "holy race," in other words, the people of God.

Because the idea of "race" seems so scientifically solid to most of us, it is helpful to know where the concept originated. One of the very earliest attempts to classify human beings according to biology and/or geography was made by Giordano Bruno and Jean Bodin in the 1500's. They distinguished between people strictly on the basis of skin color. In the 1600's, Francois Bernier developed what is believed to be the first classification of humans into distinct races: Europeans, Far Easterners, Negroes, and Lapps.[47]

In the 1700's, Carolus Linnaeus set forth a system for classifying all living things, including humans. In 1758, he published the 10th edition of *Systema Naturae*, which became the basis for scientific racism. He included not only physical characteristics and geographical location, but also other characteristics. He considered the races to be species or sub-species of the genus Homo. His classifications were:

Homo Americanus—red people; unyielding, cheerful, free
Homo Europeaus—white people; light, wise, inventor
Homo Asiaticus—yellow people; stern, haughty, greedy
Homo Africanus—black people; sly, sluggish, neglectful, lazy[48]

Others have added to and modified these original classifications by Linnaeus. In fact, the definition of race

---
47 Historical Race Concepts, n.p.
48 Charmantier, n.p.

has changed even in my lifetime. When Charlie and I were in school, we were taught that there were five races based on physical characteristics: Caucasian, Negroid, Mongoloid, Australoid, and American Indian. Charlie is of Spanish and Mexican descent, and he discovered a few years ago that some people now consider Latino or Hispanic to be a separate "race." All of a sudden, he was not white anymore!

This illustrates how capricious our definitions of race can be. And even the physical characteristics that define race are fairly arbitrary. Some members of a race do not even exhibit the physical characteristics that supposedly place them in their racial group.

Second, we agree with Critical Theory that oppression is a sin. However, our definitions of oppression are different. In the Bible, oppression is associated with violence and cruelty. In Critical Theory, oppression is determined by imposing one group's norms and values on another.[49]

Third, we can agree that power can corrupt our perception of reality. Those in power often do not perceive how the results of their actions affect others. Therefore, "Christians should approach subjects like racism, sexism, and classism with humility, recognizing that our salvation in Christ does not make us sinless or infallible interpreters of Scripture or reality."[50]

---

49   Shenvi, p. 10.
50   Shenvi, p. 10.

But again, there is a disagreement as to the cause of our flaws in perception. In Critical Theory, it is privilege and power which cause us to fail to perceive correctly. In the Bible, it is sin, which is present in the oppressor and oppressed alike.

Fourth, "hegemonic power" [dominance of one group over another] is a real phenomenon. Some people in power do impose their own values and norms on those over whom they exercise control, even without any self-serving intent. Consider early missionaries to Africa and Asia who tried to impose a European style of worship on their converts. This made many of their efforts ineffectual. Once the Gospel was associated with the culture of the native people, more and more people were willing to accept Christ.

Fifth, we can agree on the need for justice. However, biblical justice is not the same as justice as defined by critical race theorists. As Monique Duson states, "God's commands for justice are not defined by intersectionality nor do they extend only to the poor, the minority, or those identifying as LGBTQ+. The weights and measures of justice are indiscriminate."[51]

We also must be careful not to replace the Gospel with the need for justice. A graduate of Reformed Theological Seminary, Jemar Tisby, stated in an Instagram post, "Courageous Christianity dares to love through action and

---

51   Duson, n.p.

to risk everything for the sake of justice."[52] Would it not be more biblical to encourage Christians to risk everything for the sake of Christ?

WHERE CHRISTIANITY AND CRITICAL THEORY PART COMPANY

The basic problem with Critical Theory is that "it promises what it cannot deliver because it is rooted in ideas that are unbiblical."[53]

Consider some basic questions of life:

1. What are human beings?

Christianity: Human beings are created in the image of a good and loving Creator. Our primary identity comes from our relationship to Him.

Critical Theory: We are members of social groups locked in a struggle for power. Our primary identity comes from our relationship to other groups.[54]

2. What is wrong with the world?

Christianity: From the beginning of the world, humans have rebelled against God, bringing sin and suffering into the world.

---

52 Tisby, n.p.
53 Shenvi, p. 13.
54 Shenvi, p. 15.

Critical Theory: Suffering is caused by systems of oppression.[55]

3. What is necessary to change the world?

Christianity: God sent Jesus Christ to die on the cross and to be raised from the dead to rescue us from our sin.

Critical Theory: We must free oppressed groups from oppression.

4. What is our ultimate purpose?

Christianity: Our purpose in life is to glorify God and enjoy Him forever.[56] We look forward expectantly to the return of Christ when he will gather his Church, consummate all things, and establish a new heaven and new earth."[57]

Critical Theory: Our purpose in life is to fight against the subjugation of dominant groups, so that we can eventually achieve a state of equity.

5. How do we know what is true?

Christianity: "As Christians, we believe that we obtain knowledge by using reason to understand God's revelation in nature and in Scripture. When we study

---

55 Shenvi, p. 15.
56 Confessions of Our Faith, p. 124.
57 Shenvi, p. 15.

science or economics or philosophy, we are using reason to understand the works of God in the universe He created. When we study Scripture, we are using reason to understand the words of God in the Bible He inspired. Because we are sinful and because our reason and our knowledge are incomplete, our reason and knowledge will be fallible. We should always be open to correction. But if we want to understand truth, reason and logical argument are necessary tools that God has given us."[58]

Critical Theory: Members of oppressor groups are blinded by their privilege and members of oppressed groups have special access to truth that should not be challenged. Consequently, if a privileged person disagrees with the claims of the critical theorist, the critical theorist need not appeal to objective evidence or to Scripture. He can insist that the privileged person's social location has twisted their understanding and that they need to listen to and accept the claims of marginalized groups.[59]

6. What about sin?

Christianity: The Bible teaches that every human who has ever lived, with the exception of Jesus Christ, has been or is sinful. Paul tells us in Romans 3:12 that "No one does good, not even one." According to Shenvi, "The Bible insists that all Christians are held to the same

---

58 Shenvi, p. 16.
59 Shenvi, p. 16.

standards of holiness, kindness, and righteousness and that we should judge all matters impartially, favoring neither those with power nor those without. The Bible insists that – apart from the sin of Adam – each person is guilty only for sins they have personally committed."[60]

Critical Theory: Critical theorists believe that people are basically good, but that oppression can cause them to behave in harmful ways. Also, members of oppressor groups "are morally tainted by their membership in oppressor groups, irrespective of their actual thoughts, words, or deeds. Critical theorists will speak extensively about our obligation to overturn oppressive systems, to liberate the marginalized, and to seek justice, but will rarely speak about other moral virtues like honesty, kindness, chastity, patience, and forgiveness. Moreover, there are cases in which virtues like marital fidelity, modesty, or civility will be problematized as constructs of oppressor groups that need to be challenged rather than obligations that need to be honored."[61]

Note: Critical theorists hold all members of an oppressor group guilty for the deeds of the group. This differs from the Christian view of corporate sin, in which the individual members of government who imposed the sin on the nation are guilty of the sin, but the entire nation bears the consequences but not the sin itself.

---

60 Shenvi, p. 18.
61 Shenvi, p. 7

7. How does God fit into the picture?

Christianity: God is infinite, eternal, and unchangeable in His being, wisdom, power, holiness, justice, goodness, and truth.[62] He is the Creator and Sustainer of all things, both seen and unseen. Out of His infinite love, He gave His only Son as a sacrifice to atone for the sins of all who would believe. He has created a place of eternal peace and joy for those who believe in and follow Him, and He has also created a place of eternal punishment for angels and humans who refuse to accept Him.

Critical Theory: There are two possible answers.

> A. "Critical Theorists can contend that the power of a hegemonic discourse (a story the ruling class tells to justify its power) often equates with evil. A singular narrative, a singular set of values, and a singular set of norms is inherently oppressive. Because the Bible is one colossal hegemonic discourse from Genesis to Revelation, with the primary power belonging to God, God can be viewed as the ultimate oppressor."[63]

> B. Critical Theorists can also contend that because the Bible shows that God has a concern for the outsider and those who are oppressed, He could not be concerned for the oppressor. Therefore,

---
62 Confessions of Our Faith, p. 124.
63 Shenvi, p. 18.

CRITICAL THEORY

> they say God is on the side of homosexuals and transexuals; on the side of women over men; on the side of people of color over white people. They also say that if we are not working to free those outside the hegemony (dominance of one group over another), then we are not right with God, because God always stands with those outside the dominant group.[64]

FURTHER THOUGHTS ON CRITICAL RACE THEORY

A leading proponent of Critical Race Theory is Ibram X. Kendi. Two noted critics of this theory are Samuel Sey and Monique Duson. This discussion will focus on comments from Sey and Duson about Kendi's ideas.

In Samuel Sey's review of Kendi's works, he quotes Kendi as saying, "Racism is a marriage of racist policies and racist ideas that produces and normalizes racial inequities. Racial inequities exist when two or more racial groups are not standing on approximately equal footing, and a racist policy is any measure that produces or sustains racial inequity between racial groups."[65]

Therefore, according to Kendi, "A racist policy is any measure that produces or sustains racial inequity between racial groups. An antiracist policy is any measure that produces or sustains racial equity between racial groups. By policy, I mean written and unwritten laws, rules, procedures, processes,

---

64   Otten, n.p.
65   Sey, n.p.

regulations, and guidelines that govern people. There is no such thing as a nonracist or race-neutral policy. Every policy in every community in every nation is producing or sustaining either racial inequity or equity between racial groups."[66]

As Sey states, "In other words, racial disparities are always evidence of racism. Meaning, if you're not actively advocating for policies that supposedly produce racial parity at your home, school, work, or church, you're a racist. According to Kendi, if you're not attempting to end racial disparities in every setting, you're a racist. And that agenda is unmistakably Marxist. In fact, according to [Kendi's book] *How to be an Antiracist*, if you're not a Marxist, you're a racist."[67]

"Kendi is explicitly clear that antiracism is just a branch of a Marxist tree. He says: 'It is impossible to know racism without understanding its intersection with capitalism....Capitalism and racism are conjoined twins...Antiracist policies cannot eliminate class racism without anticapitalist policies.'"

According to Sey, Kendi considers anyone to be a racist if they are not radical antiracists, including some critical race theory advocates and even Dr. Martin Luther King, Jr. He considers the most threatening racist movement to be "the regular American's drive" for racial neutrality.[68]

Kendi writes, "If racial discrimination is defined as treating, considering, or making a distinction in favor or against

---
66   Kendi, n.p.
67   Sey, n.p.
68   Sey, n.p.

an individual based on that person's race, then racial discrimination is not inherently racist. The defining question is whether the discrimination is creating equity or inequity." He even advocates for segregation and racial discrimination against white people. He says, "The only remedy to racist discrimination is antiracist discrimination. The only remedy to past discrimination is present discrimination. The only remedy for present discrimination is future discrimination."[69]

Monique Duson, herself a former Critical Race Theory advocate, says, "If we follow Kendi's definition of racism through to his views on gender and sexuality, we not only see an argument that is unsettling, it is unbiblical. He writes,' To be truly antiracist is to be feminist. To truly be feminist is to be antiracist.' Later we read, 'Queer antiracism is equating all the race-sexualities, striving to eliminate the inequities between the race-sexualities.'

"These are significant statements and should be considered in light of scripture and the historic Christian worldview. Kendi's racism argument is like a quick bait and switch; we enter the conversation standing against ethnic racism and end standing up for homosexuality and transgenderism. As Christians, it is important for us to consider how we love our neighbor who may identify as LGBTQIA and simultaneously understand that we support the laws of God first. If we do not have clearly defined terms, we may find ourselves advocating for the very things that God would have us stand against."[70]

---

69   Kendi, n.p.
70   Duson, n.p.

As I have studied and analyzed Critical Theory, it has become obvious that the entire theory is based on a fatal premise—that given freedom and lack of oppression, people will naturally do good. If that were true, we would logically expect privileged white men to behave flawlessly; but there are so many examples where they haven't. Of course, that conclusion requires logical thinking, which is not required by critical theorists. They also ignore evidence provided by countries who have tried their proposals and found them to be disastrous failures. But then again, evidence doesn't matter to them either.

RatioChristi has graciously given us permission to use the quotations and paraphrases from their book *Engaging Critical Theory and the Social Justice Movement* by Neil Shenvi and Pat Sawyer. We strongly recommend that everyone download this short book. It is a free download available from Ratio Christi at ratiochristi.org/resources/publications/ or from the Center for Biblical Unity at www.centerforbiblicalunity.com.

In an interesting perspective on the application of Critical Race Theory, Billy Otten, a minister in the Presbyterian Church in America, has written a critique of a poem by Dr. Chanequa Walker-Barnes entitled "Prayer of a Weary Black Woman," which presumes many of the tenets of Critical Race Theory. Otten's article can be found in the Appendix to this book.

CHAPTER 16

SEEK MATURE CHRISTIAN WISDOM

I have a deep appreciation for Dr. Tim Keller as a church leader, church planter, author, theologian, and communicator. Additionally, his ability to give great insight into God's Word, to heighten awareness of it through powerful illustrations, and to speak wisely on various subjects is honored and admired across the world.

However, with regard to that sensitive matter of church and state, which Dr. Keller addresses in a Sept. 29, 2018 *New York Times* Op-Ed ("How do Christians fit into a two-party system? They don't.") there are other Christian leaders, like Mariam Bell, more qualified to speak and advise in this area. Bell is a Board Member for *World Magazine*, former Deputy Assistant Secretary, Department of Health and Human Services; Associate Director of Public Affairs

(Reagan Administration); National Director of Public Policy, Prison Fellowship Ministries; and Legislative Assistant, U.S. Senator Charles Grassley (R-IA).

Bell has years of legislative experience in Congress and emphasizes the importance of being both Good Samaritan and Good Watchman at the same time. Mariam Bell recently wrote "World Relief Recalls the Samaritan, but Forgets the Watchman," at the *Washington Post* concerning the signatories of a letter to President Trump and Vice President Pence (Tim and Kathy Keller were the first of 50 to sign) and published by the *Washington Post* regarding their view of the refugee resettlement. Bell noted:

- I long for them [endorsers like Tim and Kathy Keller] to seek mature Christian wisdom from all parts of the body of Christ including the watchman.

- I long to see our [church] leaders do their due diligence before signing on to public letters to the President or any policy maker for that matter.

- I want the best biblical thinkers and communicators to challenge us with a prophetic voice.[71]

In his article, Dr. Keller argues that Christians don't "fit into the two-party system" and that "they are pushed toward two main options." He also states, "Christians should not identify the Christian church or faith with a political party as the only Christian one."[72] In the past this would certainly

---
71   Bell, p. 1
72   Keller, n.p.

have been true, and there would have been no argument. However, things are different today.

For instance, when one political party in our two-party system votes into law that which is Godless in every way, and disciples others (especially our children) in this same godlessness; and when the other party does the opposite and even upholds the Moral Law of God, isn't this party the only one supporting Christian teaching? Are we not just stating the obvious? I would say it this way: where there is clear evidence that one party supports Christian values and the other party absolutely does not, and even opposes Christian values at every opportunity, does not common sense show us the foolishness of not identifying with the supporter of Christian values? Christians do not have to agree with 100% of a party platform, but they do have to agree 100% with God's Moral Law.

Dr. Keller goes on to tell a story about a man from Mississippi. Although Keller's story is interesting, I find that his use of an imprecise definition of "socialism" gives the impression that true, historic socialism is acceptable and that any political position held by other (even admirable) Christians is trustworthy:

> I know of a man from Mississippi who was a conservative Republican and a traditional Presbyterian. He visited the Scottish Highlands and found the churches there as strict and as orthodox as he had hoped. No one so much as turned on a television on a Sunday. Everyone memorized

catechisms and Scripture. But one day he discovered that the Scottish Christian friends he admired were (in his view) socialists. Their understanding of government economic policy and the state's responsibilities was by his lights very left-wing, yet also grounded in their Christian convictions. He returned to the United States not more politically liberal but, in his words, "humbled and chastened." He realized that thoughtful Christians, all trying to obey God's call, could reasonably appear at different places on the political spectrum, with loyalties to different political strategies.[73]

Keller's "man from Mississippi" was "humbled and chastened," but by what? By someone else's view of socialism? Can historic socialism really be softened, or should another term be used for what the man from Mississippi witnessed in the Scottish Highlands?

The older definition of socialism in the purest sense (e.g., North Korea and Venezuela) is "government ownership of goods and services," which is no longer a good working definition for socialism or socialistic tendencies in governments today. So rather than trying to argue from the vantage point of an outdated definition, or from a nuanced definition (what I believe Dr. Keller did), I think it is better to look at the examples and results of what happens when moving from capitalism to socialism, and then to radical socialism, which is the situation in Venezuela as Dr. Thomas Sowell writes:

---

[73] Keller

"Socialism has turned oil-rich Venezuela into a place where there are shortages of everything from toilet paper to beer, where electricity keeps shutting down, and where there are long lines of people hoping to get food, people complaining that they cannot feed their families."[74]

Are all "thoughtful Christians" trying to obey God's call, as Dr. Keller's acquaintance says? I don't think so. Otherwise "thoughtful Christians" on the Left and "thoughtful Christians" on the Right would all agree that abortion is murder; that the definition of marriage is given by God, not the state; that gender is determined by God, not the individual; that bearing false witness is very serious to God, even if our political parties don't think so. But according to Keller, "thoughtful Christians" do not agree about these things. Can both groups be right? To sacrifice biblical truth for church unity may bring about a so-called "peace in our time;" but in the long haul, it will only end in tragedy and despair.

Is it reasonable in America today to think that our two political parties, with diametrically opposing viewpoints regarding God's Moral Laws, can reach agreement without moral compromise? Such collegiality no longer exists. Today, the differences between good and evil are stark, with the one party supporting infanticide, euthanasia, gay marriage, and gender fluidity, and the list grows every day. Is it possible for "thoughtful Christians, all trying to obey God's call, to 'reasonably appear at different places on

---
[74]   Sowell, p. 1

the political spectrum, with loyalties to different political strategies?'" The answer is no, it is not possible if we honor the same God and His Word.

Consider a recent headline as an example: "Senate Democrats Fail to Protect Infants Born Alive." Should the church accept Dr. Keller's view that thoughtful Christians, all trying to obey God's call, can come to vastly different conclusions about whether the life of a child should be protected? I cannot imagine thoughtful Christians coming to any conclusion but one. If you follow Dr. Keller's advice, that would be the equivalent of saying that the Democrat Party's actions in this instance are acceptable and within the realm of Christian morality.

Tim Keller's advice might have been good advice in the past, when there was not much difference between being a Democrat or Republican. Not so when Keller wrote the article to the New York Times in 2018. To be clear, saying privately or publicly that one political party supports biblical moral values (e.g., favoring traditional marriage, sanctity of life, biological gender) and another party that does not, is not the same as saying that my church and I endorse a political party or candidate. Biblical clarity of Christian teaching is God-honoring; but denial, silence, temerity, ignorance of God's laws and man's, and fear is anything but.

The church's mission is to speak of saving grace, of sin, of common grace to everyone. This involves knowledge of God's Moral Law and action on the believers' part. This is true whether we are speaking to individuals or a group of people. When Billy Graham held a Crusade in Jackson, Mississippi, in the 1950s, he noticed upon arriving at the stadium that ropes were set up to separate blacks from whites. He did not need anyone's permission to tear them down, which he did, and warned the officials that he would leave if they were put back up. He was not afraid of the political leaders of the day because he was totally dependent upon God. He feared no man or organization in Jackson, Mississippi.

Remember the Church at Laodicea and what it was criticized for. They were "lukewarm." Laodicea in modern day terms was wealthy, but they had to pipe in their water from hot springs. The hot water was great for bathing, but when it reached Laodicea, it was lukewarm and not suitable for either bathing or drinking.

What Jesus is saying is that a lukewarm church is useless. Being useful, on the other hand, confronting corporate as well as individual sin, and showing grace, is exactly what the church should be doing all the time.

CHAPTER 17

THE MORAL OBLIGATION TO RESIST UNLAWFUL GOVERNMENT

In *A Christian Manifesto*, Francis Schaeffer argues, quoting Samuel Rutherford in *Lex, Rex,* that citizens have the moral obligation to resist unlawful government. Rutherford writes that since "tyranny is satanic, not to resist it is to resist God;" and, since the ruler is a fiduciary figure—meaning that he acts on behalf of the people—his power is not absolute, but conditional, and can be withdrawn if there is a violation of the people's trust.[75]

This applies to Christian and non-Christian rulers alike, because, as Paul stated in Romans 1:18-20, God has made Himself known to everyone. "For the wrath of God is revealed from heaven against all ungodliness and unrighteousness of men, who by their unrighteousness suppress the truth.

---
[75] Schaeffer, p. 101

For what can be known about God is plain to them. For his invisible attributes, namely, his eternal power and divine nature, have been clearly perceived, ever since the creation of the world, in the things that have been made. So they are without excuse." Simply stated, no one, even a person who has never heard of Christ or the Bible, has an excuse for doing evil, because God has revealed Himself in all of creation.

There is ample evidence—so, no excuse to the contrary—from other parts of Scripture to support resistance to a tyrannical state by the people and the church as a body:

1. Exodus 1 shows that the midwives disobeyed Pharoah
2. Exodus 1:17 says that the midwives lied to Pharoah
3. Joshua 2 says that Rahab disobeyed a command from the King of Jericho
4. 1 Kings 18 says that Obadiah defied the ruling authorities by hiding 100 prophets
5. Numerous examples given in the Book of Daniel, beginning with Shadrach, Meshach, and Abednego
6. The Book of Acts says that Peter and John refused to cease speaking about Jesus

What conclusions can be drawn from the above biblical examples? The guidelines for a Christian's civil disobedience can be summed as follows:

- Christians should resist a government that *commands*

THE MORAL OBLIGATION TO RESIST UNLAWFUL GOVERMENT 115

or *compels* evil and should work nonviolently within the laws of the land to change a government that permits evil.

- Civil disobedience is permitted when the government's laws or commands are in direct violation of God's laws and commands.

- Christians are certainly permitted to work to install new government leaders within the laws that have been established.

WHAT CAN THE CHURCH DO?

- Recognize the importance of State violations of the Moral Law.

- Accept these violations as a Church issue.

- Understand the difference between a Moral Law violation & a Social Issue.

- Accept responsibility for the most vulnerable—our children—and help parents bring them up in "the training and admonition of the Lord." (Ephesians 6:4)

- Implement a Christian Education program in your church to instruct in the moral issues of our day. Important: Moral Issues are not so-called Social Issues, and the Church must have instruction in this area.

- Seek Help to make your church stronger. I urge you to begin now. It's just that important.

CHAPTER 18

"WHEN THE DOGMA LIVES LOUDLY"

by Archbishop Emeritus of Philadelphia
Charles J. Chaput

Having previously read articles by Archbishop Chaput, I know well his caliber and ability to articulate important universally understood messages. In that sense, this article is no different. However, Archbishop Chaput says "we no longer live in a sane moment," when "civility and respect" for your belief is at play. Today, it is becoming increasingly more difficult to even use reason with antagonists. They shout you down or talk over you. However, that does not mean that we cease trying. We do, but our methods of conveying God's truth might need to change.

When Sen. Dianne Feinstein grilled federal circuit court nominee—and now Supreme Court nominee—Amy Coney Barrett three years ago, she fretted that "the dogma lives loudly within you. And that's of concern." Given the senator's obvious prejudices, she should indeed be concerned. Ms. Barrett's life story suggests that she actually believes and seeks to live what her Catholic faith teaches. Worse, she has a superb intellect, a deep grasp of the law, and an excellent record as a jurist. In other words, she's a nightmare for a certain kind of political tribe.

Let's put aside for a moment Sen. Feinstein's Know Nothing-style vulgarity. After all, she's hardly alone in her bigotry. Disdain for vigorous religious convictions, especially the Catholic kind, is a virus that's going around. It seems to infect a number of Democratic senators, including Sen. Kamala Harris, Feinstein's California colleague and vice-presidential nominee, who saw looming peril in that dangerous national conspiracy otherwise known as the Knights of Columbus.

Sen. Feinstein's words help us see clearly how some in our political class now view Catholics who are more than merely "nominal" in their faith. It's true that anyone baptized as a Catholic is, in fact, a Catholic. In the eyes of the Democratic party, that's not a problem. If you're photographed piously with your rosary beads at prayer—even better. The cultural loyalty of many Catholic voters to a once heavily Catholic, working-class party dies hard, no matter how different that party is today. As an elected official, you may even get an award from a major Catholic institution. But if you're the kind of Catholic who seeks to discipline his or her life around Catholic beliefs regarding marriage and family, religious freedom, sex, and abortion—well, that's a different matter, as Democratic Congressman Dan Lipinski discovered when his own party dumped him in a primary earlier this year. In Bill Maher's immortal words, a woman like Amy Coney Barrett, whatever her professional credentials, is just "a [expletive] nut."

In a sane age, these kinds of attacks, more appropriate to a restroom wall than discourse in a nation of laws, would be seen as loathsome. But we don't live in a sane moment, as Sens. Feinstein and Harris, and Mr. Maher, have helpfully demonstrated.

Catholics in this country spent more than a century fighting their way into the American mainstream. The cost has been high. To the degree that self-described Catholic political leaders are indistinguishable in their views and actions from their colleagues with no faith at all, the cost has been far too high. Millions of Catholics have served and died defending this nation, its freedoms, and its institutions. In the last century, all of the military chaplains awarded the Medal of Honor were Catholic priests. A politics of democratic pluralism requires that differences of belief must be respected. Catholics cannot, and don't, expect those with different convictions to agree with their religious beliefs. But Catholics *do* rightly demand civility and respect for the teachings of their Church, especially from a Senate supposedly informed by a spirit of service to the whole nation.

Today's hostility toward those who support Catholic teaching should concern every practicing Catholic—and anyone who values the First Amendment. If attacks on belief are an acceptable standard by which to impugn judicial nominees today, then tomorrow they'll be used on the rest of us who uphold the teachings of our faith. What's been playing out in Senate confirmation hearings and public debates over judicial nominees is a harbinger of future attacks on the Church herself and on any Catholic who holds with her enduring moral witness. Over the past decade, we've already seen the Catholic Church— and many of her ministries and institutions—targeted specifically for matters of belief.

Those who value our First Amendment right to religious freedom should realize that tests about belief are attacks on religious liberty. And positioning dissenting Catholics as "mainstream Americans" and believing Catholics as "extremists"—now a common and thoroughly dishonest culture war technique—is a particular affront to the free exercise of religion. It puts the rights of far more Americans at risk than will ever be nominated for the court.

Charles J. Chaput, O.F.M. Cap., is the archbishop emeritus of Philadelphia. His latest book, Things Worth Dying For: Thoughts on a Life Worth Living, *will be published by Holt in March 2021.*

©Charles Chaput. Used with permission.

CONCLUSION

Midway through this manuscript I decided to write my conclusion after watching the movie **Denial**, based on a true story about a holocaust denier who sues an Atlanta writer and her publishing company for libel. My second viewing of the movie changed my whole perspective on the worn-out phrase "separation of church and state."

Simply put, what is still taking place in the Church today when The State legislatively overturns God's Moral Law (pro-abortion legislation, redefining marriage legislation, redefining gender legislation, etc.) is not so much an issue of *silence* (my former belief), rather it is a *denial* of any responsibility to respond corporately (as a church or denomination) as well as individually.

So, whether you're a "separation of church and state" advocate, a "two kingdom" (for whatever reason) advocate, a "spirituality of the church" advocate, a "get 'em saved first and society's problems will be solved" advocate, and for those who haven't yet made up their mind, a "fill in the blank" advocate, it's all about DENIAL of RESPONSIBILITY! And any church defense such as: "Not our problem," "we weren't there," "afraid of the IRS, "too busy," "things aren't all that bad," "socialism may be more equal than capitalism (without even bothering to study its effects)," "we have pro-choice and gay Christians in our church" all beg the question because those who make these statements are assuming the validity of their arguments without comparing them to God's Word.

On the other hand, it is not a mere assertion to say that all church leaders should know the importance of the Church speaking about State violations of the Moral Law, and consequently leading the way for their congregations. This author has provided adequate proofs from Scripture, Church History, and modern research to support his argument.

Furthermore, one does not have to look very far to find tragic examples—in times of war and moral decadence—of the consequences of the Church's failure to speak clearly, and with one voice, on the issue of the State's legislative overthrow of God's Moral Law.

APPENDIX

LETTER TO A MEGA CHURCH PASTOR
Charlie Rodriguez

Recently I spoke to a staff member at a mega-church in the Dallas area regarding a letter I sent to their Senior Pastor on church and state issues. This church already does work in this area, but wanted to know more about my focus: violations of the Moral Law by State. Below is a follow-up letter I sent to the staff member summarizing points in our conversation:

Dear_____, thank you for giving me the opportunity to present an overview of my ministry, **Church and State Discussions**, to you yesterday. I hope that in the future I might be able to come alongside what is already being done at your church and offer something I am convinced will make a difference. Briefly, what this Presbyterian brother, and in the tradition of D. James Kennedy and Francis Schaeffer, can bring to the discussion are the following points (and more), which I would like to present in more detail to you and others at _____:

Most churches today still operate off of an older or "separation" model of Church and State. The idea of a newer model, which never separates out the God's Moral Law, should look something like this:

1. The moral issues of the day, imposed on us by our government, are the province of the Church to define and oversee. I emphasize that "In matters of morality the Christian Church (and not just any church) should

navigate the ship of state." In the past, and still today, the clear moral teachings of the Bible are unfortunately grouped together with many social issues of the day. There must be due diligence on the part of the Church to know and teach the difference between what typically belongs to a "social gospel" and what is unquestionably a violation of God's Moral Code.

2. In addition to what individual candidates may say privately or to a church group, more important is what the Party platform says. This is what party leaders should and do insist that its members hold to firmly. Clearly, there is no reason the Christian Church should not publicly affirm Biblical party positions from the pulpit.

3. Most recently (over the past 3 years) we have seen wholesale violations of the 9th Commandment where politicians publicly "bear false witness against a neighbor" or do so under oath (perjury) and get away with it. We need to discuss these violations, at Church as well as at home.

4. Emphasis of Common Grace is important for a number of reasons: First, it enhances the understanding of Special Grace by showing how gracious and good is our Lord. He offers Salvation through His Son, but He also "sends the rain on the righteous and the unrighteous" (Mt. 5:45). Second, Common Grace, when understood through obedience to the Moral Law, offers protection and stability in society instead of chaos.

5. Actual "Separation of Church and State" is very dangerous because it promotes separation of God's Moral Law from our daily lives. Most people want law and order, and want to live safe lives. The problem is that they don't understand what promotes it, and they don't see it as a moral issue. The Church has the proper understanding and the ability to bring about biblical/moral change, if it will accept the responsibility.

6. Churches especially need to understand that God's Moral Law has been politicized. So, it is no longer about politics as usual (or quid pro quo), it is about the Moral Code and whether our elected leaders are going to adhere to a higher law. If they say they are Christian, then they have no excuse. If they are non-Christian, Scripture teaches that still there is no excuse because God's truths are written on their hearts (Romans 2:15) and are part of their spiritual DNA or genetic code.

7. It is extremely important that the Church recognize and make known to its members which political party most nearly supports the Moral Law of God.

8. To think that God does not judge nations who reject Him is not only naive thinking (they do not understand history) but un-Scriptural as well.

10 REASONS WHY THE CHURCH SHOULD NOT ABANDON POLITICS

Jerry Newcombe

Recent events have raised the issue, Should the pulpit always avoid politics? It depends on what we mean by "politics;" it demeans the pulpit to use it for partisan politics. But here are ten reasons why I don't think politics and religions should (or even can) be completely separate.

1. **The Word of God has something to say about all of life, beyond just the spiritual.**

   My long-time pastor, Dr. D. James Kennedy, once noted that the Church of Jesus Christ has always been opposed to abortion—from the very beginning. It still is.

   In the last generation, abortion has become a "political" issue. Does that mean, asked Dr. Kennedy, we should now ignore it in the pulpit? No, because the Bible is pro-life.

2. **The Bible itself addresses the issue of governing in different texts.**

   There are biblical books dealing with political rulers—1 and 2 Samuel, 1 and 2 Kings, Judges. In Genesis and in Daniel, we see godly men serving well in pagan courts, for the good of all. In Romans 13 and 1 Peter 2, we hear that God has established the civil magistrate, and we are to obey the government. In Exodus, we see Moses rebuking Pharaoh for mistreating the Hebrews.

3. **The Scriptures also teach that on occasion, there may be a need for civil disobedience.**

   When the apostles were commanded to no longer preach the gospel, Peter said that we must obey God rather than man. If there is an either/or, then civil disobedience can be the right path. Many early Christians died for Christ rather than worship the emperor, clearly a false god.

4. **Jesus said, "Render to Caesar the things that are Caesar's, and to God the things that are God's."**

   Nature abhors a vacuum. Someone will be involved in politics. Why should we abandon our role as citizens? According to Jesus, we have a positive duty to render certain obligation to the state.

5. **When the Church does not speak out, evil can fill that void.**

   Silence in the face of evil can signal assent. We hold up those Christians who went against Hitler and the Nazis as heroes—not the millions who acquiesced to them.

   The December 23, 1940 TIME Magazine article called, "Religion: German Martyrs," opens: "Not you, Herr Hitler, but God is my Führer. These defiant words of Pastor Martin Niemoller were echoed by millions of Germans. And Hitler raged: 'It is Niemoller or I.'"

APPENDIX

6. **The Church is called to be salt and light. Salt preserves and prevents decay.**

   Christians in society should help prevent corruption. As goes the pulpit, so goes the nation.

7. **We pray, "Thy kingdom come, Thy will be done, on earth as it is in heaven."**

   That doesn't mean we should try and force the kingdom of God by use of the sword. When "Christians" did that in times past, we are still apologizing for it, as in the Crusades, the Inquisition, the Salem Witchcraft trials. But it does mean that Christians can apply biblical principles to government that result in good for all of us. And to be sure, someone's morality is always being legislated. It is not a question of "if," but of "what" and of "whose."

8. **Christians bless everybody when we properly apply our faith to politics.**

   Our Constitution was an outgrowth of the biblical concept of covenant. University of Houston Professor Dr. Donald S. Lutz, author of "The Origins of American Constitutionalism," said that Americans "invented modern Constitutionalism and bequeathed it to the world." And where did we get it? Says Lutz: "The American constitutional tradition derives in much of its form and content from the Judeo-Christian tradition as interpreted by the radical Protestant sects to which belonged so many of the original European settlers in British North America."

9. **Politics may be the calling of some in the congregation. Therefore, ministers should encourage political involvement that is motivated by the desire to serve.**

When the Member of Parliament William Wilberforce was converted in the 1780s, he sought counsel from Rev. John Newton, an ex-slave-trader. Should he leave politics and pursue the ministry? Newton advised him to stay because maybe God could use him where he was.

Wilberforce's crusade to free the slaves in the British Empire took him 50 years and was a direct outgrowth of his faith in Christ. I shudder to think if one of today's "no politics" ministers had counseled the young reborn Wilberforce. We might still have legal slavery in the Western world.

10. **Religion and morality are "indispensable supports to our political prosperity."**

So said Washington in his Farewell Address. John Adams said, "Our Constitution was made only for a moral and religious people. It is wholly inadequate to the government of any other." This was in a day when about 99% of the Americans were professing Christians. And on it goes.

APPENDIX

I remember when I once interviewed former Secretary of Education William Bennett, who said, "Does anybody really have a worry that the United States is becoming overly pious? That our young people have dedicated too much of their lives to prayer, that teenagers in this country are preoccupied with thoughts of eternity?" In short, our problem today is not too much Christian influence on society, but not enough.

Jerry Newcombe, D.Min., is an on-air host/senior producer for D. James Kennedy Ministries. He has written/co-written 31 books, e.g., The Unstoppable Jesus Christ, American Amnesia: Is American Paying the Price for Forgetting God?, What If Jesus Had Never Been Born? (w/ D. James Kennedy) & the bestseller, George Washington's Sacred Fire (w/ Peter Lillback) djkm.org@newcombejerry www.jerrynewcombe.com

©Jerry Newcombe. Used with permission.

THE PRAYER OF A WEARY BLACK WOMAN
VISTAS IN WOKE THEOLOGY
Billy Otten

Sarah Bessey has recently edited and published an anthology of prayers[, modeled after the psalms, which express a particularly woke point of view. The prayer that has made this biggest splash this past week is Dr. Chanequa Walker-Barnes' *Prayer of a Weary Black Woman*. Provocative, out of context snippets have been pasted across Twitter and Instagram, but the prayer deserves a more thoughtful analysis. In my limited space here I would like to offer some commendations and some criticisms of this prayer while also exploring the insights that it gives us into woke theology.

SUMMARY OF THE PRAYER
The snippets we've all seen are indeed provocative. The prayer opens with the line: "Dear God, please help me to hate white people." It's difficult to get more provocative than that. But we must also admit that some of the psalms and prayers that we find in Scripture are initially provocative. Dashing children upon the rocks comes to mind. Perhaps Dr. Walker-Barnes is doing something more deeply biblical than we might expect. So as responsible Christians, let's give the whole prayer a hearing.

As the prayer unfolds, we find that the author makes some qualifications. She does not wish to hate white anti-racists. These are white people who agree that white supremacy

APPENDIX 133

is a thing and have devoted their lives to eradicating it in themselves and society. These are allies. She also does not wish to hate explicit white racists. These are people who commit hate crimes. These people are "already in hell". Side note, but this is a surprising vista into woke theology. I was not aware that there was still room for God's judgment and eternal damnation within wokeism, but there it is.

The author wishes to hate the majority of white people. White people who are not anti-racist, but neither are they explicitly racist. To use her description, these are "nice people". People who would be glad to have her over for dinner but would also call the neighborhood watch if they saw a black person walking down the street. She wishes to hate them. She admits that she "[doesn't] have many relationships with people like that…" (I wonder why?). But she wishes to hate them, nonetheless.

Why? These people make her weary. They do participate in racism and white supremacy but they fail to recognize it and they are not willing to change when she calls them out. She's wearied of calling them out. She pleads with the Lord to: "Free me from this burden of calling them to confession and repentance."

The prayer then turns to a hopeful note. She recognizes that God will not allow her to hate white people. He continues to call her to love her neighbor as herself—even if that neighbor is white. She also recognizes the many ways that God has delivered her from racism and the prayer ends with a note of confidence that God will continue to do this as she continues her quest to make white people less racist.

COMMENDATIONS

We must admit that this prayer is heartfelt and creative. It's categorized as a prayer of "disorientation." The anthology is organized according to Brueggemann's popular categorization of all psalms as orientation, disorientation, or reorientation. As a prayer of disorientation (like a psalm of lament or imprecation) it does take a biblical form. It is biblical for God's people to bring requests to God even though they may not be answered in the affirmative. Jesus himself prayer that God would take the cup from him if there could be any other way. He did not want to endure the horror of the cross. Yet, in the end, he submitted to God's will. This prayer attempts to take on that biblical form and it should be commended for that.

Dr. Walker-Barnes wishes to be relieved of the burden of putting up with white people. She does not wish to bear this cross. She pleads for God to take it away from her. But when He will not, she submits to the cross of living with and loving white people. And, of course, this means taking on the prophetic role of continuing to call out the ubiquitous racism that plagues everything that white people do, say, and think. As a true martyr, she submits to this calling. Thank you, Dr. Walker-Barnes. So if I were to commend this prayer for one thing, it's that it attempts to take on a biblical form that we do not often see in prayer.

APPENDIX

CRITICISMS

First, this prayer puts Dr. Walker-Barnes (and anyone who prays it) in the position of the righteous sufferer without any acknowledgement of personal guilt. Dr. Walker-Barnes is weary of putting up with ignorant sinners (white people) around her and would be free of them. There is no sense of her own sinfulness, her own bias, her own racism, or her own need of forgiveness in this prayer. Jesus asked us how we could remove the speck from our brother's eye when there is a log in our own. At least this means that we ought to be recognizing and repenting of sin in our own lives before we try to help others escape sin. But the petitioner in this prayer does not have any sin to confess. Jesus Christ alone is the righteous sufferer. I would be uncomfortable coming to the Lord with a prayer like this without acknowledging my own guilt and my own complicity in racial disunity.

Second, this prayer assumes that a great many disagreements between the author and evangelical Christians are due to racism. This criticism is broadly true of all woke theology, but we see a particular example of this here. As she describes the white people she wishes to hate, she describes them as, "The people who welcome Black people in their churches and small groups but brand us as heretics if we suggest that Christianity is concerned with the poor and the oppressed." I must assume that she is referring to white Christians who are uncomfortable with the social gospel, i.e., white evangelicals. But this is far too simplistic. There are many prominent black theologians, pastors, and Christians who also see the social gospel as theologically deficient. Let's not dismiss evangelicals and gospel-centered Christians so easily by branding them as racists.

Finally, this prayer does nothing to help race relations. It casts nearly all white people as the enemies of God. It casts nearly all black people as friends of God. But the Bible tells us that those who have faith in Jesus Christ—no matter their ethnicity—are friends of God. We should not think that God is on the side of the oppressed no matter what. And we should not think that God is against those who are in power no matter what. This isn't Christianity. This is (of course) Marxism.

So, if you're going to critically interact with this prayer and this book, please read the whole thing. It's important to get the full context. And it's important to read and understand these voices because Intersectionality is quickly becoming the new American religion. We have to deftly navigate these thorny theologies to be able to affirm legitimate pain points but also to expose some of the poisonous fruits that grow there.

Billy Otten is a Minister in the Presbyterian Church in America and serves as Assistant Pastor of Faith PCA in Cincinnati, Ohio.

©Billy Otten. Used with permission.

APPENDIX

PREFACE TO COMMON GRACE

The following chapter, Common Grace, by Dr. Louis Berkhof, from his Systematic Theology is critical reading if we are to have a full and balanced understanding of Saving Grace. Most important in this chapter is Berkhof's summary of Calvin's position on Common Grace:

> [Calvin] developed alongside the doctrine of particular grace the doctrine of common grace. This is a grace which is communal, does not pardon nor purify human nature, and does not affect the salvation of sinners. [However] it restrains the destructive power of sin, maintains in a measure the moral order of the universe, thus making an orderly life possible, distributes in varying degrees gifts and talents among men, promotes the development of science and art, and showers untold blessings upon the children men.

Most theologians (Calvin, Kuyper, Berkhof, Sproul, Boice, Hodge,) teach God's kindness and loving provision for everyone, or Common Grace, but it is primarily Berkhof who emphasizes the necessity of having an ordered, rather than disordered, society in which to live, and that the Church plays a part in this order.

Although the Church needs to be cautious of promoting a social gospel, it must always be ready to clarify and support issues which are clearly moral in nature according to the Bible.

COMMON GRACE
Louis Berkhof

In connection with the general operations of the Holy Spirit the subject of common grace also calls for attention. It should be understood, however, that Reformed theology does not, like Arminian theology, regard the doctrine of common grace as a part of Soteriology. At the same time, it does recognize a close connection between the operations of the Holy Spirit in the sphere of creation and in that of redemption, and therefore feels that they should not be entirely dissociated.

A. ORIGIN OF THE DOCTRINE OF COMMON GRACE.

1. THE PROBLEM WITH WHICH IT DEALS.

The origin of the doctrine of common grace was occasioned by the fact that there is in the world, alongside of the course of the Christian life with all its blessings, a natural course of life, which is not redemptive and yet exhibits many traces of the true, the good, and the beautiful. The question arose, how can we explain the comparatively orderly life in the world, seeing that the whole world lies under the curse of sin? How is it that the earth yields precious fruit in rich abundance and does not simply bring forth thorns and thistles? How can we account for it that sinful man still "retains some knowledge of God, of natural things, and of the difference between good and evil, and shows some regard for virtue and for good outward behavior"? What explanation can be given of the special gifts and talents with which the natural man is endowed, and of the development of science and art by those who are entirely devoid of the new life that is in Christ Jesus? How can we explain the religious aspirations of men everywhere, even of those who did not come in touch with the Christian religion? How can the unregenerate still speak the truth, do good to others, and lead outwardly virtuous lives? These are some of the questions to which the doctrine of common grace seeks to supply the answer.

2. AUGUSTINE'S ATTITUDE TO THIS PROBLEM.

Augustine did not teach the doctrine of common grace, though he did not use the word "grace" exclusively as a designation of saving grace. He spoke of a grace which Adam enjoyed before the fall, and even admitted that man's existing as a living, sentient, and rational being might be termed grace. But over against Pelagius, who stressed the natural ability of man and recognized no other grace than that consisting in the natural endowments of man, the law and the gospel, the example of Christ, and the illumination of the understanding by a gracious influence of God, — he emphasized the total inability of man and his absolute dependence on the grace of God as an inner renewing power, which not only illumines the mind but also acts directly on the will of man, either as operating or as co-operating grace. He employs the word "grace" almost exclusively in this sense, and regards this grace as the necessary condition to the performance of each good act. When the Pelagians pointed to the virtues of the heathen, who "merely through the power of innate freedom" were often merciful, discreet, chaste, and temperate, he answered that these so-called virtues were sins, because they did not spring from faith. He admits that the heathen can perform certain acts which are in themselves good and from a lower point of view even praiseworthy, but yet considers these deeds, *as the deeds of unregenerate persons*, to be sin, because they do not spring from the motive of love to God or of faith, and do not answer to the right purpose, the glory of God.[Cf. Polman, *De Predestinatieleer van Augustinus, Thomas van Aquino en Calvijn*, pp. 77 f.; Shedd, *History of Christian Doctrine II*, pp. 75 f.] He denies that such deeds are the fruit of any natural goodness in man.

3. THE VIEW THAT DEVELOPED DURING THE MIDDLE AGES.

During the Middle Ages the Augustinian antithesis of *sin and grace* gave way to that of *nature and grace*. This was based on another antithesis which played an important part in Roman Catholic theology, namely, that of the natural and the supernatural. In the state of integrity man was endowed with the supernatural gift of original righteousness, which served as a bridle to hold the lower nature in check. As the result of the fall, man lost this supernatural gift, but his real nature remained or was but slightly affected. A sinful bias developed, but this did not prohibit man from producing much that was true, and good, and beautiful. However, without the infusion of the grace of God, all this did not suffice to give one a claim to life eternal. In connection with the antithesis of the natural and the supernatural, the Roman Catholic Church developed the distinction between the moral virtues of humility, obedience, meekness, liberality, temperance, chastity, and diligence in what is good, which men can gain for themselves by their own labors, and with the timely aid of divine grace; and the theological virtues of faith, hope, and charity, which are infused into man by sanctifying grace. Anabaptism and Socinianism suffer from the same antithesis, but with the distinction that the former exalts grace at the expense of nature, while the latter exalts nature at the expense of grace.

4. THE POSITION OF THE REFORMERS AND OF REFORMED THEOLOGY.

On this, as on some other points of doctrine, Luther did not entirely escape the leaven of Roman Catholicism. While he did return to the Augustinian antithesis of sin and grace, he drew a sharp distinction between the lower earthly sphere and the higher spiritual sphere, and maintained that fallen man is by nature capable of doing much that is good and praiseworthy in the lower or earthly sphere, though he is utterly incapable of doing any spiritual good. With an appeal to Augustine the Augsburg Confession teaches "that man's will hath some liberty to work a civil righteousness, and to choose such things as reason can reach unto; but that it hath no power to work the righteousness of God."[Art. XVIII.] The Article contains a quotation from Augustine, in which many of the good works pertaining to the present life, which the natural man can do, are named. Zwingli conceived of sin as pollution rather than as guilt, and consequently regarded the grace of God as sanctifying, rather than as pardoning, grace. This sanctifying influence, which penetrated in a measure even into the Gentile world, accounts for the true, the good, and the beautiful that is in the world. Calvin did not agree with the position of Luther, nor with that of Zwingli. He firmly maintained that the natural man can of himself do no good work whatsoever and strongly insisted on the particular nature of saving grace. He developed alongside of the doctrine of particular grace the doctrine of common grace. This is a grace which is communal, does not pardon nor purify human nature, and does not affect the salvation of sinners. It curbs the destructive power of sin, maintains in a measure the moral order of the universe, thus making an orderly life possible, distributes in varying degrees gifts and talents among men, promotes the development of science and art, and showers untold blessings upon the children of men. Since the days of Calvin the doctrine of common grace was generally recognized in Reformed theology, though it also met with occasional opposition. For a long time, however, little was done to develop the doctrine. This was in all probability due to the fact that the rise and prevalence of Rationalism made it necessary to place all emphasis on special grace. Up to the present Kuyper and Bavinck did more than anyone else for the development of the doctrine of common grace.

B. NAME AND CONCEPT OF COMMON GRACE.

1. NAME.

The name "common grace" as a designation of the grace now under discussion cannot be said to owe its origin to Calvin. Dr. H. Kuiper in his work on *Calvin on Common Grace* says that he found only four passages in Calvin's works in which the adjective "common" is used with the noun "grace," and in two of these the Reformer is speaking of saving grace. [Cf. p. 178.] In later Reformed theology, however, the name *gratia communis* came into general use to express the idea that this grace extends to all men, in contrast with the *gratia particularis* which is limited to a part of mankind, namely, to the elect. In the course of time it became evident that the term "communis" admitted of various interpretations. In Dutch theology it is often regarded as equivalent to "general," and as a result it became customary to speak of "general grace" (*algemeene genade*) in the Netherlands. Strictly speaking, however, the term *communis*, as applied to grace, while implying that it is general in some sense of the word, stresses the fact that this grace is communal, that is, possessed in common by all creatures, or by all men, or by those who live under the administration of the gospel. Thus Dr. H. Kuiper classifies the common grace of which Calvin speaks under three heads, namely: (1) Universal Common Grace, a grace that extends to all creatures; (2) General Common Grace, that is a grace which applies to mankind in general and to every member of the human race; and (3) Covenant Common Grace, a grace that is common to all those who live in the sphere of the covenant, whether they belong to the elect or not. It is quite evident that Reformed theologians also subsumed under the term "common grace" a grace that is not general, namely, the external privileges of those who are living under the administration of the gospel, including the external universal calling. At the same time they point out that this grace, in distinction from general common grace, belongs to the economy of redemption. [Cf. Mastricht,

God geleerdheit I, p. 441; Brakel, *Redelijke Godsdienst* I, pp. 729 f.; Hodge, *Syst. Theol.* II, p. 654; A. A. Hodge, *Outlines of Theol.*, p. 449; Shedd, *Calvinism Pure and Mixed*, pp. 98 f.; Vos, *Geref. Dogm.* IV, pp. 13 f.] Finally, it should be noted that the term *gratia communis* is susceptible of, and has actually received, not only a quantitative, but also a qualitative interpretation. It may denote a grace that is common in the sense of *ordinary*. The ordinary, in distinction from the special, operations of the Holy Spirit are called common. His natural or usual operations are contrasted with those which are unusual and supernatural. This is the meaning of the term "common" in the *Westminister Confession* X. 4; and the *Westminster Larger Catechism*, Q. 60. W. L. Alexander declares of the common grace enjoyed by those who live under the gospel: "The grace thus bestowed is common, not in the sense of being given to all men in common, but in the sense of producing effects which are ordinary, and may fall short of a real saving efficacy."[*System of Bib. Theol.* II, p. 352.] So understood, the grace of God may be common without being general or universal.

2. CONCEPT.

The distinction between common and special grace is not one that applies to grace as an attribute in God. There are no two kinds of grace in God, but only one. It is that perfection of God in virtue of which he shows unmerited and even forfeited favour to man. This one grace of God manifests itself, however, in different gifts and operations. The richest manifestation of it is seen in those gracious operations of God which aim at, and result in, the removal of the guilt, the pollution, and the punishment of sin, and the ultimate salvation of sinners. But while this is the crowning work of the grace of God, it is not its only manifestation. It appears also in the natural blessings which God showers upon man in the present life, in spite of the fact that man has forfeited them and lies under the sentence of death. It is seen in all that God does to restrain the devastating influence and development of sin in the world, and to maintain and enrich and develop the natural life of mankind in general and of those individuals who constitute the human race. It should be emphasized that these natural blessings are manifestations of the *grace* of God to man in general. Some prefer to say that they are expressions of His goodness, kindness, benevolence, mercy, or longsuffering, but seem to forget that He could not be good, kind, or benevolent to the *sinner* unless He were first of all *gracious*. It should be borne in mind, however, that the term *gratia communis*, though generally designating a grace that is common to the whole of mankind, is also used to denote a grace that is common to the elect and the non-elect that are living under the gospel, such as the external gospel call that comes to both alike, and that inner illumination and those gifts of the Spirit of which we read in Heb. 6:4-6. It is understood, however, that these privileges can be called common grace only in the sense that they are enjoyed by the elect and the reprobate indiscriminately, and that they do not constitute special, in the sense of saving, grace. In distinction from the more general manifestations of common grace they, while they do not constitute a part of the grace of God that necessarily leads to salvation, are nevertheless related to the soteriological process. They are sometimes called "special" grace, but then "special" is not equivalent to "saving." In general it may be said that, when we speak of "common grace," we have in mind, either (a) *those general operations of the Holy Spirit whereby He, without renewing the heart, exercises such a moral influence on man through His general or special revelation, that sin is restrained, order is maintained in social life, and civil righteousness is promoted*; or, (b) *those general blessings, such as rain and sunshine, food and drink, clothing and shelter, which God imparts to all men indiscriminately where and in what measure it seems good to Him.*

The following points of distinction between special (in the sense of saving) and common grace should be noted:

a. The extent of special grace is determined by the decree of election. This grace is limited to the elect, while common grace is not so limited, but is granted to all men indiscriminately. The decree of election and reprobation has no determining influence on it. It cannot even be said that the elect receive a greater measure of common grace than the non-elect. It is a matter of common knowledge, and has frequently been observed, that the wicked often possess a greater measure of common grace and have a greater share in the natural blessings of life than the pious.

b. Special grace removes the guilt and penalty of sin, changes the inner life of man, and gradually cleanses him from the pollution of sin by the supernatural operation of the Holy Spirit. Its work invariably issues in the salvation of the sinner. Common grace, on the other hand, never removes the guilt of sin, does not renew human nature, but only has a restraining effect on the corrupting influence of sin and in a measure mitigates its results. It does not effect the salvation of the sinner, though in some of its forms (external calling and moral illumination) it may be closely connected with the economy of redemption and have a soteriological aspect.

c. Special grace is irresistible. This does not mean that it is a deterministic force which compels man to believe against his will, but that by changing the heart it makes man perfectly willing to accept Jesus Christ unto salvation and to yield obedience to the will of God. Common grace is resistible, and as a matter of fact is always more or less resisted. Paul shows in Rom. 1 and 2 that neither the Gentiles nor the Jews were living up to the light which they had. Says Shedd: "In common grace the call to believe and repent is invariably ineffectual, because man is averse to faith and repentance and in bondage to sin."[*Calvinism Pure and Mixed*, p. 99.] It is ineffectual unto salvation because it leaves the heart unchanged.

d. Special grace works in a spiritual and re-creative way, renewing the whole nature of man, and thus making man able and willing to accept the offer of salvation in Jesus Christ, and to produce spiritual fruits. Common grace, to the contrary, operates only in a rational and moral way by making man in a general way receptive for the truth, by presenting motives to the will, and by appealing to the natural desires of man. This is equivalent to saying that special (saving) grace is immediate and supernatural, since it is wrought directly in the soul by the immediate energy of the Holy Spirit, while common grace is mediate, since it is the product of the mediate operation of the Holy Spirit through the truth of general or special revelation and by moral persuasion.

This conception of common grace should be carefully distinguished from that of the Arminians, who regard common grace as a link in the *ordo salutis* and ascribe to it saving significance. They hold that, in virtue of the common grace of God, the unregenerate man is perfectly able to perform a certain measure of spiritual good, to turn to God in faith and repentance, and thus to accept Jesus unto salvation. They go even farther than that, and maintain that common grace by the illumination of the mind and the persuasive influence of the truth incites the sinner to accept Jesus Christ and to turn to God in faith and repentance, and will certainly achieve this end, unless the sinner obstinately resists the operation of the Holy Spirit. The Canons of Dort have this in mind where they reject the error of those who teach "that the corrupt and natural man can so well use the common grace (by which they understand the light of nature), or the gifts still left him after the fall, that he can gradually gain by their good use a greater, that is, the evangelical or saving grace, and salvation itself."[III-IV. Rejection of errors 5.]

C. COMMON GRACE AND THE ATONING WORK OF CHRIST.

The question naturally arises, whether the manifestation of common grace is in any way connected with the atoning work of Christ. As far as we know, Dr. Kuyper does not posit such a connection. According to him Christ as the Mediator of creation, the light that lighteth every man coming into the world, is the source of common grace. This means that the blessings of common grace flow from the work of creation. But this hardly suffices to answer the question, how it is to be explained that a holy and just God extends grace to, and bestows favors upon, sinners who have forfeited everything, even when they have no share in the righteousness of Christ and prove finally impenitent. The question is exactly, how can God continue to bestow those blessings of creation on men who are under the sentence of death and condemnation? As far as the elect are concerned this question is answered by the cross of Christ, but how about the reprobate? Perhaps it can be said that it is not necessary to assume a specific judicial basis for the bestowal of common grace on man in view of the fact (a) that it does not remove the guilt of sin and therefore does not carry pardon with it; and (b) that it does not lift the sentence of condemnation, but only postpones the execution. Perhaps the divine good pleasure to stay the revelation of His wrath and to endure "with much longsuffering vessels of wrath fitted unto destruction," offers a sufficient explanation for the blessings of common grace.

Reformed theologians generally hesitate to say that Christ by His atoning blood merited these blessings for the impenitent and reprobate. At the same time, they do believe that important natural benefits accrue to the whole human race from the death of Christ, and that in these benefits the unbelieving, the impenitent, and the reprobate also share. In every covenant transaction recorded in Scripture it appears that the covenant of grace carries with it not only spiritual but also material blessings, and those material blessings are generally of such a kind that they are naturally shared also by unbelievers. Says Cunningham: "Many blessings flow to mankind at large from the death of Christ, collaterally and incidentally, in consequence of the relation in which men, viewed collectively, stand to each other."[*Hist. Theol.* II, p. 333.] And it is but natural that this should be so. If Christ was to save an elect race, gradually called out of the world of humanity in the course of centuries, it became necessary for God to exercise forbearance, to check the course of evil, to promote the development of the natural powers of man, to keep alive within the hearts of men a desire for civil righteousness, for external morality and good order in society, and to shower untold blessings upon mankind in general. Dr. Hodge expresses it thus: "It is very plain that any plan designed to secure the salvation of an elect portion of a race propagated by generation and living in association, as is the case with mankind, cannot secure its end without greatly affecting, for better or for worse, the character and destiny of all the rest of the race not elected." He quotes Dr. Candlish to the effect that "the entire history of the human race, from the apostasy to the final judgment, is a dispensation of forbearance in respect to the reprobate, in which many blessings, physical and moral, affecting their characters and destinies forever, accrue even to the heathen, and many more to the educated and refined citizens of Christian communities. These come to them through the mediation of Christ, and coming to them now, must have been designed for them from the beginning."[*The Atonement*, pp. 358 f.] These general blessings of mankind, indirectly resulting from the atoning work of Christ, were not only foreseen by God, but designed by Him as blessings for all concerned. It is perfectly true, of course, that the design of God in the work of Christ pertained primarily and directly, not to the temporal well-being of men in general, but to the redemption of the elect; but secondarily and indirectly it also included the natural blessings bestowed on mankind indiscriminately. All that the natural man receives other than curse and death is an indirect result of the redemptive work of Christ.[Cf Turretin, Opera, Locus XIV, Q. XIV, par. XI; Witsius, *De Verbonden*, B. II, Kap. 9, s. 4; Cunningham, *Hist. Theol.* II, p. 332; Symington, *Atonement and Intercession*, p. 255; Bavinck, *Geref. Dogm.* III, p. 535; Vos, *Ger. Dogm.* III, p. 150.]

D. THE RELATION BETWEEN SPECIAL AND COMMON GRACE.

Several questions may be raised respecting this relation, of which the following are some of the most important.

1. DO SPECIAL AND COMMON GRACE DIFFER ESSENTIALLY OR ONLY IN DEGREE?

Arminians recognize alongside of sufficient (common) grace the grace of evangelical obedience, but maintain that these two differ only in degree and not in essence. They are both soteriological in the sense that they form part of the saving work of God. The former makes it possible for man to repent and believe, while the latter, in co-operation with the will, causes man to repent and believe. Both can be resisted, so that even the latter is not necessarily effectual unto salvation. Reformed theology, however, insists on the *essential* difference between common and special grace. Special grace is supernatural and spiritual: it removes the guilt and pollution of sin and lifts the sentence of condemnation. Common grace, on the other hand, is natural; and while some of its forms may be closely connected with saving grace, it does not remove sin nor set man free, but merely restrains the outward manifestations of sin and promotes outward morality and decency, good order in society and civic righteousness, the development of science and art, and so on. It works only in the natural, and not in the spiritual sphere. It should be maintained therefore that, while the two are closely connected in the present life, they are yet *essentially* different, and do not differ merely in degree. No amount of common grace can ever introduce the sinner into the new life that is in Christ Jesus. However, common grace does sometimes reveal itself in forms that can hardly be distinguished by man from the manifestations of special grace as, for instance, in the case of temporal faith. Dr. Shedd does not seem to bear the essential difference between

APPENDIX

the two in mind especially when he says: "The non-elect receives common grace, and common grace would incline the human will if it were not defeated by the human will. If the sinner should make no hostile opposition, common grace would be equivalent to saving grace." In a note he adds: "To say that common grace, if not resisted by the sinner, would be equivalent to regenerating grace, is not the same as to say that common grace, if assisted by the sinner, would be equivalent to regenerating grace. In the first instance, God would be the sole author of regeneration; in the second He would not be."[*Dogm. Theol.* II, p. 483.] This reminds one of Lutheran theology, but the author's meaning is not entirely clear, for elsewhere he also ascribes the non-resistance of the sinner to the operation of the Holy Spirit.[*Calvinism Pure and Mixed*, p. 101.]

2. WHICH ONE OF THE TWO IS PRIMARY, COMMON OR SPECIAL GRACE?

To this question it must be answered that in a temporal sense neither one of them can be said to be prior to the other. The third chapter of Genesis clearly reveals that both of them go into operation at once after the fall. Logical priority should be ascribed to special grace, however, because common grace is made subservient to this in its operation in the world.

3. DOES COMMON GRACE SERVE AN INDEPENDENT PURPOSE OR NOT?

It cannot be doubted that common grace finds its purpose in part in the redemptive work of Jesus Christ; it is subservient to the execution of the plan of God in the life of the elect and in the development of the Church. But in addition to that it also serves an independent purpose, namely, to bring to light and to harness for the service of man the hidden forces of nature, and to develop the powers and talents that are latent in the human race, in order that man may ever-increasingly exercise dominion over the lower creation, to the glory of God the Creator.[Cf. Kuyper, *Gemeene Gratie* II, pp. 622, 628, 633; Bavinck, *De Algemeene Genade*, p. 45.]

4. DO SPECIAL AND COMMON GRACE EACH HAVE A PECULIAR SPHERE ENTIRELY DISTINCT FROM THAT OF THE OTHER?

It may be said that in a certain sense special grace has its own peculiar sphere in the organized Church, though it is not necessarily limited to this, and common grace is also operative in the Church for it is granted to all men. Both operate in the world, but while common grace in the more usual sense of the term pertains to the things of the natural world and this present life, special grace bears on the things of the new creation. They cannot but influence each other. Common grace enriches the Church with its blessings; and the Church raises the fruits of common grace to a higher level by bringing them under the influence of the regenerate life.

E. THE MEANS BY WHICH COMMON GRACE OPERATES.

Several means can be distinguished by which common grace effects its work. Calvin suggests some of these when he, in speaking of the restraining influence of common grace says: "Hence, how much soever men may disguise their impurity, some are restrained only by shame, others by fear of the laws, from breaking out into many kinds of wickedness. Some aspire to an honest life, as deeming it most conducive to their interest, while others are raised above the vulgar lot, that, by the dignity of their station, they may keep inferiors to their duty. Thus God by his providence, curbs the perverseness of nature, preventing it from breaking forth into action, yet without rendering it inwardly pure."[*Inst.* II. 3,3.] The following are some of the most important means through which common grace effects its work.

1. THE LIGHT OF GOD'S REVELATION.

This is fundamental for without it all other means would be impossible, and even if possible, would fail to function properly. We have in mind here primarily the light of God's revelation that shines in nature and lightens every man coming into the world. It is itself the fruit of common grace, but in turn becomes a means for the further manifestation of it, since it serves to guide the conscience of the natural man. Paul speaks of the Gentiles who do by nature the things of the law, "in that they show the word of the law written in their hearts, their conscience bearing witness therewith, and their thoughts one with another accusing or else excusing them." Rom. 2:14,15. Calvin in commenting on this passage says that such Gentiles "prove that there is imprinted on their hearts a discrimination and judgment by which they distinguish between what is just and unjust, between what is honest and dishonest."[*Comm. on Romans in loco.*] In addition to this, however, it may be said that common grace in a more restricted sense also operates in the light of God's special revelation, which is not itself the fruit of common, but of special, grace.

2. GOVERNMENTS.

Of these too it may be said that they are at once the fruit and the means of common grace. According to Rom. 13 governments are ordained of God, to maintain good order in society. To resist them is to resist the ordinance of God. The ruler, says Paul, "is a minister of God to thee for good." Rom. 13:4. He finds support in the conscience of man (verse 5) and for the rest "beareth not the sword in vain." On this point the Belgic Confession says: "We believe that our gracious God, because of the depravity of mankind, hath appointed kings, princes, and magistrates, willing that the world should be governed by certain laws and policies; to the end that the dissoluteness of men might be restrained, and all things carried on among them with good order and decency."[Art. XXXVI.]

3. PUBLIC OPINION.

The natural light that shines in the hearts of men, especially when re-enforced by the influence of God's special revelation, results in the forming of a public opinion that is in external conformity with the law of God; and this has a tremendous influence on the conduct of men who are very sensitive to the judgment of public opinion. Naturally public opinion will be a means of common grace only when it is formed under the influence of God's revelation. If it is not controlled by conscience, acting in harmony with the light of nature, or by the Word of God, it becomes a mighty influence for evil.

4. DIVINE PUNISHMENTS AND REWARDS.
The providential arrangements of God, whereby He visits the iniquity of men upon them in this life, and rewards deeds that are in outward conformity with the divine law, serve an important purpose in curbing the evil that is in the world. punishments have a deterring effect, and the rewards serve as incentives. By these means, whatever there is of moral goodness in the world is greatly encouraged. Many shun evil and seek that which is good, not because they fear the Lord, but because they feel that good brings its own reward and best serves their interests.

F. THE FRUITS OF COMMON GRACE.

In the preceding it was already intimated that what is left to us of the light of nature, is still operative only in virtue of the common grace of God. It is one of the most important fruits of common grace, without which some of the others would not be conceivable. The following fruits may be mentioned here:

1. THE EXECUTION OF THE SENTENCE IS STAYED.
God pronounced the sentence of death on the sinner. Speaking of the tree of the knowledge of good and evil, He said. "In the day that thou eatest thereof thou shalt surely die." Man did eat of it, and the sentence went into execution to a certain extent, but clearly was not fully executed at

once. It is due to common grace that God did not at once fully execute the sentence of death on the sinner, and does not do so now, but maintains and prolongs the natural life of man and gives him time for repentance. He does not at once cut short the life of the sinner, but affords him an opportunity to repent, thereby removing all excuse and justifying the coming manifestation of His wrath upon those who persist in sin unto the end. That God acts on this principle is abundantly evident from such passages as Isa. 48:9; Jer. 7:23-25; Luke 13:6-9; Rom. 2:4; 9:22; II Peter 3:9.

2. THE RESTRAINT OF SIN.

Through the operation of common grace sin is restrained in the lives of individuals and in society. The element of corruption that entered the life of the human race is not permitted, for the present, to accomplish its disintegrating work. Calvin says: "But we ought to consider that, notwithstanding the corruption of our nature, there is some room for divine grace, such grace as, without purifying it, may lay it under internal restraint. For, did the Lord let every mind loose to wanton in its lusts, doubtless there is not a man who would not show that his nature is capable of all the crimes with which Paul charges it, (Rom. 3 compared with Ps. 14:3 ff)."[*Inst.* II. 3,3.] This restraint may be external or internal or both, but does not change the heart. There are passages of Scripture which speak of a striving of the Spirit of God with men which does not lead to repentance, Gen. 6:3; Isa. 63:10; Acts 7:51; of operations of the Spirit that are finally withdrawn, I Sam. 16:14; Heb. 6:4-6; and of the fact that in some cases God finally gives up men to the lusts

APPENDIX

of their own hearts, Ps. 81:12; Rom. 1:24,26,28. In addition to the preceding passages there are some which are clearly indicative of the fact that God restrains sin in various ways, such as Gen. 20:6; 31:7; Job 1:12; 2:6; II Kings 19:27,28; Rom. 13:1-4.

3. THE PRESERVATION OF SOME SENSE OF TRUTH, MORALITY AND RELIGION.

It is due to common grace that man still retains some sense of the true, the good, and the beautiful, often appreciates these to a rather surprising degree, and reveals a desire for truth, for external morality, and even for certain forms of religion. Paul speaks of Gentiles who "show the work of the law written in their hearts, their conscience bearing witness therewith, and their thoughts one with another accusing or else excusing them," Rom. 2:15, and even says of those who gave free vent to their wicked lives that they knew the truth of God, though they hindered the truth in unrighteousness and exchanged it for a lie, Rom. 1:18-25. To the Athenians, who were devoid of the fear of God, he said, "Ye men of Athens, in all things I perceive that ye are very religious," Acts 17:22. The Canons of Dort express themselves as follows on this point: "There remain, however, in man since the fall, the glimmerings of natural light, whereby he retains some knowledge of God, of natural things, and of the difference between good and evil, and shows some regard for virtue and for good outward behavior. But so far is this light of nature from being sufficient to bring him to a saving knowledge of God and true conversion that he is incapable of using it aright even in things natural and civil.

Nay, further, this light, such as it is, man in various ways renders wholly polluted, and hinders in unrighteousness, by doing which he becomes inexcusable before God." III-IV. 4.

4. THE PERFORMANCE OF OUTWARD GOOD AND CIVIL RIGHTEOUSNESS.

Common grace enables man to perform what is generally called *justitia civilis*, that is, that which is right in civil or natural affairs, in distinction from that which is right in religious matters, natural good works especially in social relations, works that are outwardly and objectively in harmony with the law of God, though entirely destitute of any spiritual quality. This is in harmony with our Reformed Confession. Art. XIV of the Belgic Confession speaks in its title of man's incapacity to perform what is truly good, says that man retained only small remains of his excellent gifts, so as to render him without excuse, and rejects only the Pelagian error that man can of himself perform spiritual or saving good. The Canons of Dort III-IV, Art. 3, speak in a similar vein: "Therefore all men are conceived in sin, and are by nature children of wrath, incapable of saving good" etc. It may be objected that the Heidelberg Catechism speaks in absolute terms when it says in Question 8 that we are incapable of doing any good unless we are regenerated. But it is quite evident from the Commentary of Ursinus himself that he would not deny that man can do civil good, but only that he can perform good works such as are defined in Question 91 of the Catechism. Reformed theologians generally maintain that the unregenerate can perform natural good, civil good, and outwardly religious good.[Cf.

Calvin, *Inst.* III. 14,2; Van Mastricht, *Godgeleerdheid*, Bk. IV. 4,11,12; Voetius, *Catechisatie* I, p. 168-172; Ursinus, Comm. on the Catechism, Lord's Day II, p. 77; Charnock, *On the Attributes* II, pp. 303,304; Brakel, *Redelijke Godsdienst* I, p. 338.] They call attention to the fact, however, that, while such works of the unregenerate are good from a material point of view, as works which God commanded, they cannot be called good from a formal point of view, since they do not spring from the right motive and do not aim at the right purpose. The Bible repeatedly speaks of works of the unregenerate as good and right, II Kings 10:29,30; 12:2 (comp. II Chron. 24:17-25); 14:3,14-16,20,27 (comp. II Chron. 25:2); Luke 6:33; Rom. 2:14,15.

5. MANY NATURAL BLESSINGS.

To common grace man further owes all the natural blessings which he receives in the present life. Though he has forfeited all the blessings of God, he receives abundant tokens of the goodness of God from day to day. There are several passages of Scripture from which it appears abundantly that God showers many of His good gifts on all men indiscriminately, that is, upon the good and the bad, the elect and the reprobate, such as: Gen. 17:20 (comp. vs. 18); 39:5; Ps. 145:9,15,16; Matt. 5:44,45; Luke 6:35,36; Acts 14:16,17; I Tim. 4:10. And these gifts are intended as blessings, not only for the good but also for the evil. In the light of Scripture the position is untenable that God never blesses the reprobate, though He does give them many gifts which are good in themselves. In Gen. 39:5 we read that "Jehovah blessed the Egyptian's house for Joseph's sake; and the blessing of

Jehovah was upon all that he had in the house and in the field." And in Matt. 5:44,45 Jesus exhorts His disciples in these words, "Bless those that curse you . . . that ye may be children of your Father who is in heaven." This can only mean one thing, namely, that God also blesses those who curse Him. Cf. also Luke 6:35,36; Rom. 2:4.

G. OBJECTIONS TO THE REFORMED DOCTRINE OF COMMON GRACE.

Several objections have been and are even now raised by some against the doctrine of common grace as it is presented in the preceding. The following are some of the most important of these:

1. Arminians are not satisfied with it, because it does not go far enough. They regard common grace as an integral part of the saving process. It is that sufficient grace that enables man to repent and believe in Jesus Christ unto salvation, *and which in the purpose of God is intended to lead men to faith and repentance,* though it may be frustrated by men. A grace that is not so intended and does not actually minister to the salvation of men is a contradiction in terms. Hence Pope, a Wesleyan Arminian, speaks of common grace in the Calvinistic system as "being universal and not particular; being necessarily, or at least actually, inoperative for salvation in the purpose of God," and calls this a "wasted influence." He further says: "Grace is no more grace, if it does not include the saving intention of the Giver."[*Christian Theology* II, pp. 387 f.] But, surely, the Bible does not so

limit the use of the term "grace." Such passages as Gen. 6:8; 19:19; Ex. 33:12,16; Num. 32:5; Luke 2:40, and many others do not refer to what we call "saving grace," nor to what the Arminian calls "sufficient grace."

2. It is sometimes argued that the Reformed doctrine of common grace involves the doctrine of universal atonement, and therefore leads into the Arminian camp. But there is no good ground for this assertion. It neither says nor implies that it is the purpose of God to save all men through the atoning blood of Jesus Christ. The objection is based particularly on the universal proclamation of the gospel, which is considered possible only on the basis of a universal atonement. It was already suggested by the Arminians themselves at the time of the Synod of Dort, when they asserted that the Reformed with their doctrine of particular atonement could not preach the gospel to all men indiscriminately. But the Synod of Dort did not recognize the implied contradiction. The Canons teach particular atonement,[II. 8.] and also require the universal proclamation of the gospel.[II. 5 and III. 8.] And this is in perfect harmony with Scripture, which teaches on the one hand, that Christ atoned only for the elect, John 10:15; Acts 20:28; Rom. 8:32,33; cf. also John 17:9; and on the other hand, that the gospel call must be extended to all men indiscriminately, Matt. 22:2-14; 28:19; Mark 16:15,16. If it be objected that we cannot fully harmonize the indiscriminate and sincere offer of salvation on condition of faith and repentance with the doctrine of particular atonement, this may be admitted but with the distinct understanding that the truth of a doctrine does

not depend on our ability to harmonize it with every other doctrine of Scripture.

3. Another objection to the doctrine of common grace is that it presupposes a certain favorable disposition in God even to reprobate sinners, while we have no right to assume such a disposition in God. This stricture takes its starting point in the eternal counsel of God, in His election and reprobation. Along the line of His election God reveals His love, grace, mercy, and longsuffering, leading to salvation; and in the historical realization of His reprobation He gives expression only to His aversion, disfavor, hatred, and wrath, leading to destruction. But this looks like a rationalistic over-simplification of the inner life of God, which does not take sufficient account of His self-revelation. In speaking on this subject, we ought to be very careful and allow ourselves to be guided by the explicit statements of Scripture rather than by our bold inferences from the secret counsel of God. There is far more in God than we can reduce to our logical categories. Are the elect in this life the objects of God's love only, and never in any sense the objects of His wrath? Is Moses thinking of the reprobate when he says: "For we are consumed in thine anger, and in thy wrath are we troubled"? Ps. 90:7. Does not the statement of Jesus that the wrath of God *abideth* on them that obey not the Son imply that it is removed from the others when, *and not until*, they submit to the beneficent rule of Christ? John 3:36. And does not Paul say to the Ephesians that they "were by nature children of wrath even as the rest"? Eph. 2:3. Evidently the elect can not be regarded as *always* and *exclusively* the objects of God's

APPENDIX

love. And if they who are the objects of God's redeeming love can also in some sense of the word be regarded as the objects of His wrath, why should it be impossible that they who are the objects of His wrath should also in some sense share His divine favor? A father who is also a judge may loathe the son that is brought before him as a criminal, and feel constrained to visit his judicial wrath upon him, but may yet pity him and show him acts of kindness while he is under condemnation. Why should this be impossible in God? General Washington hated the traitor that was brought before him and condemned him to death, but at the same time showed him compassion by serving him with the dainties from his own table. Cannot God have compassion even on the condemned sinner, and bestow favors upon him? The answer need not be uncertain, since the Bible clearly teaches that He showers untold blessings upon all men and also clearly indicates that these are the expression of a favorable disposition in God, which falls short, however, of the positive volition to pardon their sin, to lift their sentence, and to grant them salvation. The following passages clearly point to such a favorable disposition: Prov. 1:24; Isa. 1:18; Ezek. 18:23,32; 33:11; Matt. 5:43-45; 23:37; Mark 10:21; Luke 6:35: Rom. 2:4; I Tim. 2:4. If such passages do not testify to a favorable disposition in God, it would seem that language has lost its meaning, and that God's revelation is not dependable on this subject.

4. Anabaptists object to the doctrine of common grace, because it involves the recognition of good elements in the natural order of things, and this is contrary to their

fundamental position. They regard the natural creation with contempt, stress the fact that Adam was of the earth earthy, and see only impurity in the natural order as such. Christ established a new supernatural order of things, and to that order the regenerate man, who is not merely a renewed, but an entirely new man, also belongs. He has nothing in common with the world round about him and should therefore take no part in its life: never swear an oath, take no part in war, recognize no civil authority, avoid worldly clothing, and so on. On this position there is no other grace than saving grace. This view was shared by Labadism, Pietism, the Moravian brethren, and several other sects. Barth's denial of common grace seems to be following along these same lines. This is no wonder, since for him too creaturliness and sinfulness are practically identical. Brunner gives the following summary of Barth's view: "It follows from the acknowledgment of Christ as the only saving grace of God that there exists no creative and sustaining grace which has been operative ever since the creation of the world and which manifests itself to us in God's maintenance of the world, since in that case we should have to recognize two or even three kinds of grace, and that would stand in contradistinction with the singleness of the grace of Christ. . . . Similarly, the new creation is in no wise a fulfilment but exclusively a replacement accomplished by a complete annihilation of what went before, a substitution of the new man for the old. The proposition, *gratia non tollit naturam sed perficit*, is not true in any sense but is altogether an arch-heresy."[*Natur und Gnade*, p. 8.] Brunner rejects this view and is more in line with the Reformed thought on this point.

QUESTIONS FOR FURTHER STUDY: Do the Hebrew and Greek words for 'grace' always denote saving grace? Are they ever used as a designation of what we call 'common grace'? Does the doctrine of common grace presuppose the doctrine of universal atonement? Does it imply a denial of the fact that man is by nature subject to the wrath of God? Does it involve a denial of man's total depravity, and of his inability to do spiritual good? Is the good which the natural man can do good only in the sight of man or also in the sight of God? Does the doctrine of common grace destroy the antithesis between the world and the kingdom of God? If not, how do you explain this?

LITERATURE: Calvin, Institutes II. 2 and 3; Kuyper, *De Gemeene Gratie*; Bavinck, *De Algemeene Genade*; ibid., *Calvin and Common Grace* (in, Calvin and the Reformation); Shedd, *Calvinism Pure and Mixed*, pp. 96-106; ibid., *Dogm. Theol.* I, pp. 432, 435; II, pp. 483 ff.; Hodge, *Syst. Theol.* II, pp. 654-675; Vos, *Geref. Dogm.* IV, pp. 11-17; Alexander, *Syst. of Bib. Theol.* II. pp. 343-361; *Discussions*, pp. 282-313 *(God's Indiscriminate Proposals of Mercy)*; H. Kuiper, *Calvin on Common Grace*; Berkhof, *De Drie Punten in Alle Deelen Gereformeerd*; Hepp, Art. *Gemeene Gratie in the Christelijke Encyclopaedie*.

From Louis Berkhof's Systematic Theology, Part Four, Chapter 3 (pp. 415-444), Wm. B. Eerdmans Publishing Co., Grand Rapids, MI

☙ This work is in the public domain in its country of origin and other countries and areas where the copyright term is the author's life plus 100 years or fewer.

BIBLIOGRAPHY

"18 U.S. Code § 1111 - Murder." Legal Information Institute. Cornell University Law School, n.d. https://www.law.cornell.edu/uscode/text/18/1111#:~:text=Murder%20is%20the%20unlawful%20killing%20of%20a%20human%20being%20with%20malice%20aforethought.&text=Whoever%20is%20guilty%20of%20murder,of%20years%20or%20for%20life.

Anderson, James. "You Shall Not Bear False Witness." Ligonier Ministries. Ligonier Ministries, June 1, 2015. https://www.ligonier.org/learn/articles/you-shall-not-bear-false-witness/.

Bell, Mariam. "World Relief Recalls the Samaritan but Forgets the Watchman." *Christian Post*, February 27, 2017.

Berkhof, Louis. "Common Grace." Essay. *In Systematic Theology*, 432–46. Grand Rapids, MI: William B. Eerdmans, 1939.

Blumbert, Naomi, Tommy Curry, and Brian Duignan. "Critical Race Theory." Britannica. Encyclopedia Britannica, June 2016. https://www.britannica.com/topic/critical-race-theory.

Bordeau, John. "Restitution and Implied Contracts." *American Jurisprudence*, Thomson West.

Chaput, Archbishop Charles. "When the Dogma Lives

Loudly." First Things. Institute on Religion and Public Life, September 28, 2020. www.firstthings.com/web-exclusives/2020/09/when-the-dogma-lives-loudly.

Charmantier, Isabelle. "Linnaeus and Race." The Linnean Society of London, 2021. https://www.linnean.org/learning/who-was-linnaeus/linnaeus-and-race#:~:test=Linnaeus'%20division%20into%20four%20varieties,%20 America%2C%20Asia%20 and%20Africa.

The Confessions of Our Faith. Fortress Edition. Clinton, MS: Fortress Book Service and Publishers, 2007.

Dennis, Gill. *Walk the Line*. Film. United States, 2005.

Duson, Monique. Web log. *Chantal Monique Duson, Founder and Racial Unity Advocate* (blog). Center for Biblical Unity, n.d.

"Fetal Development: Stages of Growth." Cleveland Clinic. Cleveland Clinic, 2021. https://my.clevelandclinic.org/health/articles/7247-fetal-development-stages-of-growth.

Frame, John. *Kingdom Theology*, email, March 18, 2021.

Frame, John. *Kingdom Theology*, email, April 22, 2021.

Frame, John. "When We Have No Recourse." Essay. In *Statism II: Solemnly Warn Them*, edited by Charlie Rodriguez. Clinton, MS: Tanglewood Publishing, 2016.

Gjelton, Tom. "The Johnson Amendment in Five Questions and Answers." NPR. National Public Radio, February 3, 2017. www.npr.org/2017/02/03/513187940/the-johnson-amendment-in-five-questions-and-answers.

Hake, Laura, and Clare O'Connor. "Genetic Mechanisms of Sex Determination." Scitable. Nature Education, 2008. Genetic Mechanisms of Sex Determination.

"Historical Race Concepts." Wikipedia, April 20, 2021.

"International Guidelines for the Determination of Death – Phase I." May 30-31, 2012 Montreal Forum Report. World Health Organization, October 2012. https://www.who.int/patientsafety/montreal-forum-report.pdf.

Jeremias, Joachim. *Jerusalem In the Time of Jesus.* Minneapolis, MN: Fortress Press, 1975.

Keller, Tim. "How Do Christians Fit Into a Two-Party System? They Don't." New York Times. New York Times, September 29, 2018. www.nytimes.com/2018/09/29/opinion/sunday/christians-politics-belief.html.

Kendi, Ibram X. "Ibram X. Kendi Defines What It Means to Be an Antiracist." Extracts. Penguin, June 9, 2020. https://www.penguin.co.uk/articles/2020/june/ibram-x-kendi-definition-of-antiracist.html.

Krauthammer, Charles. *Things That Matter.* New York, NY: Crown Forum, 2013.

BIBLIOGRAPHY

Kruger, Michael. "What Is Progressive Christianity?" RTS Wisdom Wednesday with Dr. Michael Kruger. Reformed Theological Seminary, November 3, 2020. rts.edu/resources/what-is-progressive-christianity/.

Lankford, James, and Russell Moore. "The Real Meaning of the Separation of Church and State." *Time*, Time USA, 16 Jan. 2018, 7:00 AM, time.com/5103677/church-state-separation-religious-freedom/.

Lewis, C. S. "Preface to the 1961 Edition." Essay. In *The Screwtape Letters: Annotated Edition*, xxxvii. New York, NY: Harper Collins, 1996.

Lewis, C. S. *The Screwtape Letters.* New York, NY: Harper One, 2015.

Lewis, Danny. "The Oldest-Known Carving of the Ten Commandments." *Smithsonian Magazine*, November 1, 2016.

Lockyer, Herbert. *Illustrated Dictionary of the Bible.* Nashville, TN: Thomas Nelson, 1986.

Lucas, Sean. "Owning Our Past." Reformed Faith and Practice. Reformed Theological Seminary, May 1, 2016. https://journal.rts.edu/article/owning-our-past-the-spirituality-of-the-church-in-history-failure-and-hope/.

"Martin Niemöller: First They Came For the Socialists..." *Holocaust Encyclopedia.* United States Holocaust Memorial Museum, March 30, 2012.

https://encyclopedia.ushmm.org/content/en/ article/martin-niemoeller-first-they-came-for-the-socialists?parent=en%2F10764&gclid=C j0KCQjw1PSDBhDbARIsAPeTqremTDkWZg5V ejt_CzIgQX4SHRLnJiZEmDFmAA3Q79hqBq-Phy3UufIaAoDvEALw_wcB.

Milton, Michael A. *Foundations of a Moral Government: A New Annotated Version of Lex, Rex*. Clinton, MS: Tanglewood Publishing, 2019.

"Navy Music." Naval History and Heritage Command. United States Navy, March 16, 2021. https://www.history.navy.mil/browse-by-topic/heritage/customs-and-traditions0/the-navy-hymn1.html.

Neusner, Jacob. *From Politics to Piety: The Emergence of Pharisaic Judaism*. Hoboken, NJ: Prentice-Hall, 1973.

Newcombe, Jerry. "10 Reasons Why the Church Should Not Abandon Politics." Jerry Newcombe: For God and Country, 2015. www.jerrynewcombe.com/ten-reasons-church-not-abandon-politics/.

Nirala, Satyavrat, Kara Rogers, and Gaurav Shukla. "JOHANN FRIEDRICH BLUMENBACH." Britannica. Encyclopedia Britannica, July 20, 1998. https://www.britannica.com/biography/Johann-Friedrich-Blumenbach.

NIV Study Bible. Grand Rapids, MI: Zondervan, 1985.

Otten, Billy. "Critical Race Theory." Lecture notes.

Pelikan, Jaroslov. *The Vindication of Tradition: 1983 Jefferson Lecture in the Humanities.* New Haven, CT: Yale University Press, 1984.

Schaeffer, Francis. *A Christian Manifesto.* Crossway, 1981.

Sey, Samuel. "How to Be a Racist." Slow to Write, December 19, 2020. https://slowtowrite.com/how-to-be-a-racist/.

Shenvi, Neil, and Pat Sawyer. *Engaging Critical Theory and the Social Justice Movement.* Ratio Christi, n.d. file:///C:/Downloads/E-Book-Engaging-Critical-Theory-and-the-Social-Justice-Movement.pdf.

Slade, Peter. *Open Friendship in a Closed Society: Mission Mississippi and a Theology of Friendship*, Oxford, England: Oxford University Press, 2009.

Sowell, Thomas. "Socialism a Beacon for the Gleefully Uninformed." *The Atlanta-Journal Constitution*, 3 Sept. 2016.

Sproul, R. C. "Joshua." *Ligonier Ministries*, www.ligonier.org/learn/devotionals/joshua-18/.

Stedman, Ray. "Avoiding Congregational Gangrene: 2 Tim. 2:14-19." *Ray Stedman Authentic Christianity*, 28 Mar. 1982, www.raystedman.org/new-testament/timothy/avoiding-congregational-gangrene.

Strom, Kay Marshall. *Once Blind: The Life of John Newton.*

Westmont, IL: Intervarsity Press, 2008.

Swindoll, Chuck. "Flexibility." Crosswalk.com, August 18, 2017. www.crosswalk.com/devotionals/todays-insight-chuck-swindoll/today-sinsight-august-18-2017.html1.

Tisby, Jemar. "Jemar Tisby." Instagram, January 30, 2021.

Tweeddale, John. "The World." *Tabletalk*, May 2016.

Wilberforce, William. *Real Christianity*. Bloomington, MN: Bethany House Publishers, 2006.

www.ingramcontent.com/pod-product-compliance
Lightning Source LLC
Chambersburg PA
CBHW071428160426
43195CB00013B/1843